CHRISTIAN
FOUNDATIONS

KEITH MALCOMSON

DEDICATION

To the next generation—to our nephews and nieces: Mark, Lynne, Daniel, Rebekah, Luke, Michali, Asher, Demetrius, Alanna and Kate.

That you may all come to know the one real, true, living God, Jesus Christ, as your personal Lord and Saviour, and walk with Him all your days.

CONTENTS

Hebrews 5:11–6:9

"Of whom we have many things to say, and hard to be uttered, seeing ye are dull of hearing. For when for the time ye ought to be teachers, ye have need that one teach you again which be the first principles of the oracles of God; and are become such as have need of milk, and not of strong meat. For every one that useth milk is unskilful in the word of righteousness: for he is a babe. But strong meat belongeth to them that are of full age, even those who by reason of use have their senses exercised to discern both good and evil. Therefore leaving the principles of the doctrine of Christ, let us go on unto perfection; not laying again the foundation of **repentance** *from dead works, and of* **faith toward God,** *Of the* **doctrine of baptisms,** *and of* **laying on of hands,** *and of* **resurrection of the dead,** *and of* **eternal judgment.** *And this will we do, if God permit. For it is impossible for those who were once enlightened, and have tasted of the heavenly gift, and were made partakers of the Holy Ghost, And have tasted the good word of God, and the powers of the world to come, If they shall fall away, to renew them again unto repentance; seeing they crucify to themselves the Son of God afresh, and put him to an open shame. For the earth which drinketh in the rain that cometh oft upon it, and bringeth forth herbs meet for them by whom it is dressed, receiveth blessing from God: But that which beareth thorns and briers is rejected, and is nigh unto cursing; whose end is to be burned. But, beloved, we are persuaded better things of you, and things that accompany salvation, though we thus speak."*

PREFACE

The following eight chapters were eight messages which I preached in Limerick City, Ireland, in between travels to other nations, in the latter half of, 2012. They would have remained only for those in attendance at those Bible studies if it were not for the fact that my wife, Candace, whilst listening to the recorded messages, was stirred in heart to put these messages into print, and into the hands of those who will be greatly helped, encouraged and challenged by them.

It is her diligent work in transcribing these messages and in encouraging me of the need to put them in print that has led to the production this book. My gratitude and thanks go to my wonderful and faithful friend who is my constant helpmeet in the work of the Lord. If you in any way receive true spiritual help from this book, I know much thanks must go to her in being faithful to a genuine God-given burden.

I can honestly say that more than twenty years of preaching experience was poured into these messages. The wisdom of lessons learnt from walking with Christ in wonderful fellowship and communion for more than 35 years since a child, was also poured out when they were preached. As I have re-read these chapters several times, I have become absolutely convinced of the great need for the Church to take heed to the message contained within this book. I send it forth to you with a deep longing and desire that the Church of Jesus Christ may be sanctified through the Word of God.

One final note as we embark on these messages: For decades there has been a strong dispute over the identity of the author of Hebrews, but I am confident that Paul the apostle did write it and I take that for granted throughout this book. However, I have inserted an Appendix at the end of the book with proof for the penman, Paul. I certainly would not want this issue to distract you in any way as you read because our priority is to hear the Spirit of God speak to our hearts as He reveals the wonderful person of Jesus Christ.

Keith Malcomson
March 2014
Limerick, Ireland

CHAPTER 1

FOUNDATIONS

The believer's life is often compared to the construction of a building and the first and most important part of a building is the foundation. **The size, weight, and height of a building will depend on the depth, width, and materials of the foundation.** One only lays a foundation if one intends to build a house and the purpose of building a house is to have a place to live in. Likewise, the purpose of laying in these Christian foundations is that Christ may dwell in us and live His life through us in the way He desires.

Jesus talks about a man who did not count the cost of building a house. He poured all his money into the foundation but had no funds left to build the house. Jesus said that that man was like the man who calls himself Christ's disciple; he begins to follow Christ but he does not take up his cross in order to do so and he does not forsake all in his pursuit of Christ (Lk.14:27-30, 33). We ought not build a foundation and just walk off. Again, the reason for taking such care over these foundations is so that Christ may live His life through us.

There are **six fundamentals of the faith** or **six Christian foundations** which are set forth in **Hebrews 6:2-3**. If I asked you to list what you thought were the six 'Fundamentals of the Faith' you would most likely not list most of the things which the Bible presents to us here. You would not think of them as 'fundamental'. You may think some are for the more mature only, or you may think that some are so elementary that they are not even fundamental. But here in Hebrews chapter 6 we are given six absolutely vital doctrines that we need to have built into our foundations. We will not mature or go on to perfection if they are not in place. These six doctrines must be established in our life, in our church and in our families if we want to move on to deeper things. God cannot take us on to deeper things if these basic foundations are not there.

The Six Foundational Doctrines are:
1. Repentance from dead works
2. Faith toward God
3. The doctrine of baptisms (note: plural, baptisms!)
4. Laying on of hands
5. The resurrection of the dead
6. Eternal judgment

These are the 'ABCs' of our faith. Every Christian must know these, must be taught in them, and these truths must be soundly established in every believer. If you hear a mature believer say that they have no further need of repentance for things they have done wrong, it just reveals that they have lost their foundation. They may say they are filled with the Spirit, they may speak in tongues and they may even prophesy, but in denying the need to repent, they prove that they do not have this foundation correctly laid into their lives. Their character, attitude, and lifestyle will reflect this. No one can say that this is too basic for them.

THE EPISTLE TO THE HEBREWS

This letter to the Hebrews is about Jesus Christ. Every book in the New Testament speaks about Christ, points to Christ and expounds Christ. It is a letter written to the Hebrews who were born into Judaism but born-again into Christ. They would have had a background in the Temple with all the Jewish worship, ordinances and the priesthood but had come out of that through faith in Christ.

For a Jew to be born-again is just like a Roman Catholic coming out of Catholicism and being converted. They suddenly see that all the rituals and outward observances are just mere things of the eye and the ear—mere shadows—and they realize that it is all about the person of Christ in whom they can have a real spiritual experience. In Catholicism the priest was a mediator between you and God but the convert finds out that it is not about a priest standing there in his black robe; it is about

Christ who is the true Mediator.

In this book of Hebrews the Holy Spirit repeats certain words:
- The word *Heaven* (s) 17 times
- The word *Eternal* 15 times
- The word *Perfect* 14 times
- The word *Better* 13 times

This tells me that Paul is writing about an experience of Christ that is **heavenly**. He is not just writing about the earthly ministry of Christ or a miracle that Christ did on the streets of Jerusalem—he is saying, "I want to take your eyes off the Christianity that you have your eyes on; I want you to get your eyes off 'churchianity'; off outward worship; of the doing of things; good deeds; trying to live right. I want your eyes to come off your testimony from 20 years ago, or two months ago, and I want you to set your eyes on Christ."

Christianity is not that He saved you; your testimony is not the centre of your Salvation—Christ is the centre of your salvation. The focus is not the strength of your faith: it is not, "My faith is strong!", or, "My faith is weak". No, it is Christ who is your salvation. If your trust and confidence is in meeting together, Christian fellowship, in lifting your hands in worship or in doing some good deed, you are very foolish. Paul is writing to these converted Jews who had been saved many, many years previously—even decades before. Many of them would have seen that first revival on the day of Pentecost in Jerusalem. Now Paul writes to them to exhort them to set their eyes on something **heavenly**, something **eternal,** something **perfect** and something **better** than what they have experienced in their old religion.

He writes of a better persuasion (6:9), a better priesthood (7:7), a better hope (7:19), a better covenant (7:22), better promises (8:6), better sacrifices (9:23), a better reward (10:35), a better country (11:16), and a better resurrection (11:35). Paul is saying that **to be in Christ is better than anything you have experienced** in your religion or in the world. If you think of everything you experienced outside of Christ, it is absolutely nothing in comparison to being in Christ. Nothing is as great as Christ. Religion brings burdens, fears and confusion, but in Christ there is a glorious salvation.

We long and desire that Christ is the centre of every message. Let the preacher be hidden but let Christ be seen. We do not want to preach a doctrine, a theology, a methodology or a strategy—we want Christ to be the centre and focus of everything. This is the reason for Paul writing this letter.

He writes in chapter five, verse 11, *"Of whom we have many things to say, and hard to be uttered, seeing ye are dull of hearing."* Remember Paul is writing to mature believers but he is saying that there are many things he would like to say to them (indeed he wrote this also to the Corinthians). He says there are many things he desires to preach, or to open up from the Word of God to them, but he says there is something lacking in them. It is not because Paul lacks ability, or cannot preach or teach on it, but he says, "There is something in you that hinders these revelations coming forth. Oh yes, you are saved and you know that Christ saved you; you know about the Cross and you know about being born-again; but there is something within you that is hindering the Word of God."

Do you know that God wants to speak to you at times but He withholds Himself because of where you are at? Do you know that there are things that God would open up as a divine revelation that would impact your life, change areas of your life but He has got to withhold Himself because you are not in a place to receive it? That is why it is so important to be hungry, to desire and to be in earnest when you gather to hear God's Word. If you come in apathetic God will meet you on that basis but if you come in desperate, longing, desiring and forgetting about any preacher, and just saying, "Oh, God! I need to hear from you!" God will respond to that heart. It is not all down to the preaching or the preacher. It is not all down to the ministry or the ability of the one ministering to open up the Scriptures. Very often it is down to the heart of the individual who is listening.

Paul is saying that there are many things he wants to say that are *"hard to be uttered"* which literally means 'difficult to explain.' He wants to speak to them about Christ, not a theology or a certain aspect of doctrine. He wants to tell them of deeper things concerning Christ and move them from where they are into a deep place of revelation concerning Christ, specifically His High Priestly ministry, not His earthly ministry, but His ministry now within the veil in Heaven. We have much to learn about Christ's ministry now in Heaven. We know very little compared to what He wants to reveal. The Holy Spirit here wants to reveal a mighty revelation of Christ and Paul says that some of these things are hard to explain. Even Peter said of Paul's teaching, that he teaches, *"...some things hard to be understood"* (II Peter 3:16). That word *'hard,'* (*hermeneuo*) means difficult to explain, to translate, or to interpret.

We have no right to simplify the Bible. We cannot take the Bible and say that all Biblical teaching is meant to be so simple that anybody can understand it. That is not true. You are going to have to give diligence and attention to understand some of these things in the Bible. They do not just roll off the page. They are not given to the lazy or to the person who could care less. There is truth in the Bible which will only be given to those who are diligent to study and who have a longing to learn.

When I was young I had very bad dyslexia and could hardly tell the difference between 'b' and 'd' but I longed for the Word of God and was diligent over the Word. I could barely read a chapter of the Bible before going to sleep at night, but I had a hungry heart and said, "Oh, God! Open this book to me. I want to learn the things concerning you, not academically but with this heart and this spirit of mine." And God answered that desire. No one is disqualified. No one can say, "I'm just a simple person. I'm not educated. I'm not academic" or "I'm not a person of books and studies," because we must all study the person of Christ and what the Bible says concerning Him. **This is, or should be, your entire goal in life: to learn Jesus Christ** (Eph.4:20). Nothing can hinder that apart from your own slackness and lethargy.

Paul says that they are *"...dull of hearing"* (Heb 5:11). This word *'dull,'* means to be sluggish, lazy, or slothful. Paul wants to teach them and to reveal more of Christ. But they are not able to understand and are not moving on in their Christian walk. The reason for this is that they are slothful and lazy about the things of God. Sadly we are prone to give more diligence to other things like our houses, hobbies, recreation, or sport. People go to college for years and study diligently for an exam, but do not give the same diligence to the Word of God. Is it any wonder then that we find ourselves lacking? We ought to be a student—from the youngest to the oldest—we ought to be a student of the Bible or scholar of the Word of God. For all Eternity we will be speaking about the Word and for all Eternity we will be singing the songs of the Bible.

The influx of new Bible versions in every language and nation comes from a misguided cry to see the Word of God brought down to the people's level.

When we read in the Good News Version about Shadrach, Meshach and Abednego and the threat made against them that if they did not bend down and worship the statue that they would be thrown in the fire, it translates the words of these young godly men as, *"...If God whom we serve **is able** to save us from the blazing furnace and from your power, then he will."* Now stop right there. That is heresy. Such a corrupted translation infers that they do not know if He has the power or the ability to save them; whereas it actually says: *"...our God whom we serve is able to deliver us from the burning fiery furnace, and he will deliver us out of thine hand..."* (**Dan.3:17** KJV).

As a young man I had an intelligent, older man (a preacher), sit beside me in a fellowship meeting and when he saw that I was using a King James Bible, he began to make fun of me. He laughed and joked and said, "Son, you need to get rid of that old Bible and get a proper one." After 20 minutes of his foolish jesting, I stopped him and said, "When I was young I had dyslexia yet I don't have a problem with the 'thee's' and 'thou's' or words like sanctification, justification or redemption. What's your problem?" I then went on to point out to him in his Good News Bible the above scripture in Daniel. He went rather red, ceased his foolishness, and stopped talking to me.

The whole pressure in the Church in this hour is to simplify everything in such a carnal way as to leave converts as babes. Most of the Church has become babes. Our secular school systems do quite the opposite. In primary school we know water as 'water,' but in High School we are taught that it is 'H2O'. The aim is not to bring education down to the level of the child, but rather to bring the child up to the level of education. Every subject studied at school goes in that direction, but in the Church we want to bring everything down to the youngest or simplest believer. If you cannot understand such words as justification, redemption and sanctification then give me just thirty minutes and a little bit of study and you will understand, but the question is *do you want to understand?*

Please note, I am not talking about neglecting to be sensitive to new Christians or taking time to explain something to a new believer, because that is very important, but I am talking about going on in Christ. There is a deeper revelation in Jesus Christ which is not for the lazy, not for the slothful and not for the sluggish, but it is for those who are really hungry for Jesus Christ.

Paul says, seeing *"ye are dull of hearing"* which means **you have become** *"dull of hearing";* in other words, you were not always like this. Remember he is talking to **mature believers** and he is saying you were not always *sluggish.* There was a time you were zealous over the Word of God; you burned for the Word of God but somehow through some set of circumstances or the passing of years you have gained this *sluggishness.* You have become lazy with the passing of the years. Paul is dealing with real things; with spiritual immaturity in the Hebrews.

Now, we know the Bible says it is normal to be called a babe when you are first born-again, but no one likes to be called a babe if you are mature in years. However, if you really are a babe in Christ, that is a delightful thing. There is nothing more delightful than a new baby. It cannot do all the things that adults can do; a baby cannot speak, cannot write, cannot communicate but its very giggle delights us. It would be very strange for a baby to be initially talking 'ten to the dozen', but an hour will come when its parents will expect it to talk, and so on. But Paul here is talking to these Hebrews and saying that because of their dullness and laziness, they have 'lost an edge off' their Christian life and have become babes again. They have head knowledge and a great variety of spiritual experiences, they can talk about their born-again experience, or their baptism in the Holy Spirit, or what they used to do for God, but he says they have become sluggish in their walk with God. He urges them to press on and to know more of Christ. Is your heart burning for Christ? Are you going on to perfection? Are you going on to deeper places of maturity in Christ? Do you even care about those things?

Paul gives three marks of spiritual immaturity:
1. dullness towards the Word (verse 11)
2. inability to share the Word (verse 12)
3. unskilful (inexperienced) and undiscerning in using the Word (verses 13-14)

Notice the first mark is, *'dullness toward the WORD'*, not just a general dullness to life, or others around you. It is an attitude to the Word of God. Show me a believer's attitude to the Word of God, and I will tell you many things about them. If you are devouring the Word, that says a lot, but if you have a very slack attitude toward it, relying on a past experience, then you need to be woken up.

The second mark is an, *'inability to share the Word'*. *"For when for the time ye ought to be teachers, ye have need that one teach you again which be the first principles of the oracles of God..."* (Heb 5:12). A sign of maturity is that you long to convey the truth of God to others, whether to a sinner or a saint. You long that others go deeper. Show me someone who has lost that edge and you will show me someone who does not desire to take others deeper. Why would they if they are not going there themselves? How can you take someone somewhere if you are not going there yourself? I cannot take you to Dublin if I am not going there. I might suggest that you go there for a visit, but I will not be any real help to you unless I can take you there. I will really encourage you though, if I say, "Come with me. Sit in that seat. I am going to drive you there." Many Christians like to just give directions: "Just keep going down the road 10 miles." But it is another thing altogether to say, "I am going there. Just follow me. Come with me. I am longing, desiring, and hungering after God."

If on a Sunday you hear a Word but do nothing with it—you don't go back to the Scriptures to mull it over and you do not share it with anyone or give it to any one—it does not, and will not profit you anything. We should meditate on the messages we are hearing week by week. We should carry the message into the Prayer meeting and begin to pray them. We should carry them into our own secret closet. We should be going back to the Scriptures after Sunday and should begin to

8

study those same Scriptures on Monday, Tuesday, and Wednesday. Those things we noted down which God spoke to us, we should desire to return to. Something will happen in your spiritual walk when you begin to do that.

Christians who go to meeting after meeting and do not recall what they have heard, who do not pray it through, and do not go back and study it, are at best just maintaining, but they certainly are not moving on. They are treading water but not gaining ground or going anywhere. In actual fact to stand still is to go back. You can be sure that if you are just attempting to maintain you are losing ground and going back.

You may say, "I seemed impacted on Sunday morning, but cannot remember what was preached by Sunday night." There are no less than five warnings given in the book of Hebrews concerning our attitude toward the Word of God. In Hebrews 2, it talks about, giving, *"more earnest heed to the things which we have heard, lest at any time we should let them slip."* There is a very explicate picture behind this Greek word for *slip*. It literally means, 'lest you are like a boat tied to the river bank by a rope which comes loose, because of the flow of the river, and the boat starts to float down the river.' It is a casual letting go of the Word of God and being carried along by the flow. That is a bad attitude to have toward the Word of God. "Yes, we heard the Word of God, but there it goes…there'll be another sermon next Sunday. There it goes…but there will be another along shortly." This is an attitude of the heart. You have become lazy over the Word of God.

The third mark of spiritual immaturity, is being **unskilful or inexperienced or being undiscerning in using the Word**. It is fine for a babe to be like that. A young believer does not discern all things. A young believer does not understand all things and does not have experience in all things—there is much for you to move forward in which is exciting. But a new believer should be standing on their tiptoes with excitement as they taste and find the things of God to be so good. There should be a longing for more.

Again these marks of spiritual immaturity are fine if you are a young convert, but after a year of grounding something has to begin to happen. If you are saved more than three years and those marks of immaturity are coming in on you, you must wake up and give diligence to the Word of God. We are not playing games with the Word of God. **We will be held accountable for the messages we have heard.** Jesus said, *"Take heed how you hear..."* (Luke 8:18). We are not taught in churches HOW to hear the Word of God. We are taught, "Come, and be here!" but we are not taught HOW to hear the Word of God. You are going to have to DO something with what you hear. You will be held accountable.

What would my wife say if every meal time I come to the table and say, "Beautiful meal?" I sit there, look at it, stare at it, enjoy looking at it, smelling it and even say, "Thank you very much," but I walk away without eating it or feeding on it and never digest it. I may have enjoyed the smell, the sight, the moment of sitting there and thinking, "WOW, that must have taken some labour!" but I walk away every meal time. Two things will happen: I will die and she will be very upset. My wife cannot be satisfied to put a meal out every meal time, three times a day every day, and see me not eat it. At some point she will say, "Hold on now. Sit down. We need to talk about this!"

Many people are like that in the churches. They used to be here, but they are gone now—they 'fell out the back door.' They never fed themselves on the Word of God. They were not pressing on in Christ. They came to a standstill and before long they were going backwards and then 'fell out the back door.' Be careful of someone who one minute is sitting on the front row, earnest and eager, saying, "This is unbelievable!" with their Bible in hand, but the next minute they are on the back row with Bible closed and the 'burning' has gone. That zeal and passion is lost. Something happened.

Young believers, be prepared and do not misunderstand this, for at some point you will come into a meeting and *feel* nothing; you will not be burning like you used to and you are going to ask, "What is wrong with me?" but at that time you need to walk by faith, not by sight and not by feelings.

Paul lays out the difference between those that are *babes* and those that are of *full age* who are mature or perfect. He says the milk of the Word is for babes and the milk is these foundations which we are going to study. The important thing to note though about milk is that **adults still drink milk; milk is not only for babies**. You will never stop taking milk but if milk is all I am drinking and eating, then I will be a very skinny, malnourished man who will not have sufficient energy for living. I need various foods to survive as a mature, grown man. We all need to hear these foundations again and again and those who are newly saved need them firmly in place in order to grow.

Babe	Milk	Foundations
Full age	Strong meat	Going on to perfection

Peter writes, *"As newborn babes, desire the sincere milk of the word, that ye may grow thereby"* (I Pet.2:2). That word 'desire' used here means to 'earnestly desire' or 'intensely crave after.' That is a very strong expression. This speaks of the new Christian who has an intense, burning, longing for the milk of the Word which is the elementary teachings of the Word. A 'babe' is born with this desire. If you are born-again and you have no desire for the Word, you had better put a big question mark over your experience. Peter is saying that we are **all** to desire earnestly or to crave after, *"the sincere milk of the word."* You should be crying, "Feed me! Bring these doctrines on! I want to be fed by them. I am craving them!—even the doctrine of Repentance. I am craving to hear about faith toward Christ. I long to hear about these things that I might feed myself and become strong."

In Hebrews 5:12, Paul calls these foundational doctrines the *"first principles of the oracles of God."* The word *"first"* (*arche*) means commencement or beginning. The word *"principles"* (*stoicheion*) means to be arranged in order. The word *"oracles"* (*logion*) means an utterance. Paul is speaking of that which is the beginning, the commencement of everything given in words by God and laid out in order. Every believer must go through the process of building these vital, primary teachings into their lives. Every believer must know them with their mind, receive them with their heart, and practically work them out in their Christian life. How can you go on to deeper things if these foundations are not in place?

Paul is saying to the Hebrews that they should be teachers

by now, but instead they need to be taught repentance again. Many in the church need to be taught repentance again—they have forgotten it; they have become lazy and lost the reality of repentance and that is why they are not moving on. We need to tell them to sit down and learn the message of repentance again.

We need to check our foundations and be sure they are in good repair, because if there is anything wrong with those foundations it will manifest in your thoughts, in your attitudes, in your lifestyle and if you are not pressing on hard in Christ, it is time to go back to the foundations.

For the new believer, the whole Christian life will be determined by the foundations. In twenty years time your entire Christian walk, where you are in Christ, will be determined by how these foundations are laid in now, therefore give yourself earnestly to these teachings.

Paul also calls them (6:1), *"the principles of the doctrine of Christ."* In other words this is the beginning truths of your relationship and your walk with Christ. You will not know Christ the High Priest, or know Him in all His depths and fullness if you do not know Him in these six doctrines. This is the teaching and truth of Christ.

That word 'doctrine' which is used here is the Greek word, *logos,* which means 'something said' and is the same as John 1:1, *"In the beginning was the Word* [logos]*, and the Word* [logos]*, was with God, and the Word* [logos]*, was God."* Jesus Christ is the living *logos.* Your Bible is the written *logos.* Both are called the *logos,* which is why you can never separate the written Word from Jesus Christ who is the living embodiment of the written logos. The Bible is the revelation of Christ. Before there was a Bible, a preacher or a prophet, there was Christ, the *logos*, but in time He was placed in the written Scriptures. The Bible is not just ink on a page. **The Bible is authoritative over your life because it is the Word of God**. If you want to know the mind of Christ about anything or God's will for your life, it is there in the Word. If you want to know the character of Christ, it is there. If you soak yourself in the Word, you will know Jesus Christ. If this becomes a vital part of you and is written on your mind and written on your heart, if you feed on the Word of God, then more and more of Christ will be in you, and you will become more like Him as your mind is changed to think like Him. It is impossible to devour the Word and remain the same. **Do not ever make a separation between the Bible and Christ.**

Jesus said, *"If you love me, keep my commandments..."* (Jn 14:15). If you do not keep Christ's commandments you do not love him.

"But I love Jesus!"

"No you do not if you do not keep His commandments!" Your love is determined or revealed by your obedience. If you obey Him, then you love Him. If you do not obey Him, then you do not love Him.

Today when we talk about keeping His commandments we hear the cry of 'legalism', but Jesus said to keep His commandments. It is not a case of trying to be good enough for God but as a born-again believer I have a desire to live for Him in obedience to His commands. I want to follow Him. If something is wrong, I do not want to do it, and if something is right, I want to do it. That is a simple desire put in my heart by the grace and the mercy of God.

In chapter six, verse one, Paul talks about, *"the foundation"* or *themelios,* which means 'something put down, that is, a substructure of a building.' There is no house without the foundation. Repentance is at the foundation.

Do not talk about preaching or ministry for God; do not talk about a thousand things that you are going to do for God because you had a dream or a prophecy. If you are serious about God using you in your lifetime, then you are going to take heed to the foundations and make sure that the foundations are in good repair. Checking these foundations tells me that you want God to use you. A lazy Christian is not sanctified and when he wants to go out on the streets with you to evangelize, or offers to do something in the church, they have every other sort of motive than that of Christ. This is why there are so many problems in today's Church: we want people to labour for Christ and do things for Christ but they do not have good foundations!

B.H. Clendennen used to say, "I don't mind using a baby bottle to feed a new believer, but if I have to take out the false teeth to do it, I do mind! There is something seriously wrong then!"

In other words if a Christian who is still a babe after ten, twenty or thirty years, there is something wrong with their spiritual foundations. To grow is normal. A parent would be very worried if their child did not grow. If a child stops growing, we need to find out why. Sadly we neglect this as Christians. We should be asking, "Why aren't you pressing on? Why aren't all the desires and longings there?" We tend to say, "That's just the way they are." Oh no! It is a reflection of their spiritual state and the condition of their heart. It is often said, "They are just carnal." Yes, they are carnal, but no believer has an excuse.

With some people Christ examines the foundation and says, "Right we'll get you to Heaven, but I cannot use you. What am I going to fill with my glory? How could I use such an unprepared vessel to bring revival?" You only believe in revival if you are building a house for God to fill. You give Him a house and He will come and fill it. There is no point saying, "The foundations are down, now, Lord, send a revival so that everything can be built!" No! **God is looking for a prepared people.**

You reveal your attitude to God by laying these foundations and checking these foundations. How you respond to repentance, faith and these other foundational teachings will determine how you will walk as a Christian in the future.

WHEN THE FOUNDATIONS ARE ONLY 'TASTED'

Hebrews 6:4-6, gives us a dreadful picture of how a man can experience God yet fall into apostasy. Paul writes, *"For it is impossible for those who were once enlightened, and have **tasted** of the heavenly gift, and were made partakers of the Holy Ghost, And have **tasted** the good word of God, and the powers of the world to come, If they shall fall away, to renew them again unto repentance; seeing they crucify to themselves the Son of God afresh, and put him to an open shame."*

John Bunyan, in *Pilgrim's Progress,* draws a picture for us of this man. He describes him as a man in an iron cage. Pilgrim is brought into a room, where he sees a man in a metal cage who is groaning and moaning. He is a prisoner, held captive in a cage so small he can hardly move. Pilgrim asks, "What am I looking at? Who is this man?" and the Interpreter begins to explain that this is a man who has had many spiritual experiences, but he has fallen from grace and fallen away from God. He knows everything; he can tell you about many spiritual experiences but he does not have God. He is a prisoner. Pilgrim tries to encourage the man to believe, but he says he cannot believe. He admits that once he could believe but now he can no longer believe. Pilgrim encourages him to repent, but the man once again says he cannot, moreover he has no desire to repent. He recognizes that he has passed the point of repentance.

That man in the cage knows everything that a believer 'a long time on the road,' ought to know. That man had everything of the fundamentals of the faith taught to him, for it says he was *"once enlightened."* It does not say he was justified, sanctified, born-again or even saved; none of those terms were used and I point this out because it says that, *"...it is impossible..."* for this man to be renewed. A backslider (like the Prodigal Son) by God's grace CAN be renewed. God does not need to give us a second chance, but because He is so gracious and merciful, He does. However, this man in the cage is not just a backslider because it says *it is impossible* to renew this man and of course we know it *is* possible for a backslider to be renewed. This man was:

1. A man whose mind was *"once enlightened";* he once understood the Gospel. His eyes were opened enough to say, "I see! I see! I need Christ!"
2. A man who *"tasted of the heavenly gift"* but it does not say he ate it or drank it. Christ is that heavenly gift to us.
3. *"A partaker"* of the Holy Ghost which means he associated himself with the Holy Ghost or had a share in workings and movings of the Spirit. This is just like Saul (of the Old Testament) on whom an evil demon came making him so angry he wanted to kill. Then after this the Spirit of God came on him and he prophesied with the prophets. Too often in today's Church we have people who are not born-again but who are prophesying. It is possible for the real Holy Ghost to come upon wicked men who then give real prophecy. Balaam is another example of a man who truly prophesied by the real Spirit, yet was not right with God.

4. A man who *"tasted the good word of God".* Again he tasted but did not devour it; he never fed on it.
5. A man who tasted of *"the powers of the world to come"* He experienced something of the power of eternity, of the unseen world to come and of Heaven on Earth.

This man *tasted* these many things. In other words, he had many, many spiritual experiences of Christ, the Holy Ghost and the Word of God but he fell away. When it speaks of 'falling away' (*parapipto*) it means to fall away from the side of something or someone. It is a slipping, sliding or wandering off; a falling away from the right way. To *fall away from the side of* is to fall away from the side of Christ; the side of God's Word; from the fellowship of the saints. It begins with an initial straying and moving away. Be very careful. This is what the Bible calls apostasy from God. At the point when Pilgrim meets him, he is outside of Christ and he knows it. He has no faith and no desire to repent of his sin or take hold of the Word of God or at least is unable to.

Saints, we ought to stir up our hearts to take a hold of these things. Do not take your salvation for granted. Give more earnest heed to these things. Do not be slack over what God does for you. Woe unto you if you treat your salvation lightly.

The point of this teaching in Hebrews is not to cause fear but to exhort all true believers to keep moving forward in their growth in Christ. Please remember that Paul is especially speaking to the babes—the ones who have stopped growing— saying, "Come on saints, grow!" and he is also speaking to the new converts, saying, "Lay these foundations in!"

Remember, Peter, writes in his second epistle, *"And beside this, giving all diligence, add to your faith virtue; and to virtue knowledge; And to knowledge temperance; and to temperance patience; and to patience godliness; And to godliness brotherly kindness; and to brotherly kindness charity"* (II Peter 1:5-7). Peter writes that you should lay these things in because if you do, *"ye shall never fall"* (verse 10). **If you want to be preserved from falling then GROW and keep growing!** Desire to keep growing and you will not fall.

Paul goes further in verses 7-8, *"For the earth which*

drinketh in the rain that cometh oft upon it, and bringeth forth herbs meet for them by whom it is dressed, receiveth blessing from God: But that which beareth thorns and briers is rejected, and is nigh unto cursing; whose end is to be burned" (Heb.6). An apostate is like ground which receives rain but only produces thorns and briers. Here is ground upon which rain has fallen. The apostle paints a picture here of two pieces of ground: one is like a true believer and one is like this man in the iron cage. The same rain has fallen on both the good and the wicked. They have the same experiences, which means that both are given the same opportunities, the same benefits and promises, yet one of them bears good fruit and one of them bad fruit. One of them will be blessed of God and the other cursed to an eternal Hell. One of them is like this man caught up in a spiritual experience—he is not a sinner out there on the streets and he is not an atheist—he has had a real experience with God, yet he is far away from God and from living in the truth of God.

Peter also speaks about this kind of man or woman and compares them to pigs and dogs (II Pet.2:22). They are NOT BACKSLIDERS, but they are those who once knew the things of God but have gone off and lived their own life. They are like pigs brought in, thoroughly washed, and scrubbed, but soon after being washed they return to rolling in the mud because that is the NATURE of the pig. The nature of that pig was never changed. **It may have been washed but it is still a pig.** It may have looked good for a time and you could even have had the pig in your house for a little time but by its nature it desires that mud (a picture of the man who desires to return to his sin). Peter, then by describing a dog returning to its vomit, reiterates that it is in the nature of the dog to do that. The very thing which made that dog sick, the dog desires to take back into its belly.

These are serious things. The blessings of God may be very evident in the Church, the preaching may go forth, but two men or women may sit in the same meeting, side by side, both saying, "Amen! Praise the Lord! We believe this!" yet one of them **by their lifestyle** will later prove that they believed nothing and have no desire to be conformed to Jesus Christ while the other grows in Christ and goes on to perfection. These two great apostles are saying that it is better not to know the way of righteousness, than to turn from it.

In Luke 8:13, Christ says, *"...when they hear [the word of God, they] receive the word with joy; and these have no root,* [foundation] *which for a while believe, and in time of temptation fall away."* Notice, they received the Word with great joy. And with joy they say, "I can't believe this! I can't believe what Christ has done for me! Thank you, Lord, for your mercy!" But just two weeks or two months down the road, they are not willing to separate from the world and sin. When they start to hear the cost of following Christ and when temptations come, trials come, they are gone. They only believed for a short time because they had no root in them. It was not a case of the foundations crumbling or the roots failing, it is that they never had any roots or foundations.

The word which Christ uses here for, *'fall away'* is *aphistemi* which means: to remove; to actively instigate to a revolt; to desist, desert, depart or withdraw; a removal from being established; to be moved from standing; he with whom you once stood, you now rebel against. They once seemed to be a friend of Christ, but now reveal that they are enemies of Christ.

If you establish good roots in Christ you will still be here in five years time and still learning more of Jesus Christ. Saints, when you are truly rooted in Christ you can be assured that a thousand years from now you will be worshipping at His throne of glory. Do not lose that desire.

It is said of Simon the Sorcerer (Acts 8), that *he believed* and was then baptized in water. Everywhere that you saw Philip the Evangelist, you saw Simon beside him. Simon wanted to be identified with the preacher. Peter and John came to that revival to pray for them to be brought into the baptism in the Holy Ghost and Peter took one look at Simon and the gifts of the Holy Spirit began to operate. Now, do not forget that Philip thought that Simon was 'ok' and that Simon was a good convert. Philip saw a man whose life had changed; who was no longer doing witchcraft in Samaria; who was not leading people into false doctrine anymore. This was a man sitting in the front row of church. Philip no doubt thought that Simon loved the preaching of the Word, but Peter said to Simon, *"For I perceive that thou art in the gall of bitterness, and in the bond of iniquity"* (8:23).

He was a child of the Devil. Simon was washed like the pig but his nature had not been changed; his character was not changed; he was not born-again. He was intimately joined to iniquity—not Christ.

Christ, said that there were those that believed on Him when they saw the miracles (Jn.2:23-24). They were sure that Christ was the Messiah because they saw the miracles and maybe even experienced a personal healing—they believed on Him because of the miracles, but Christ knew what was in their hearts so He did not commit Himself or entrust Himself to them. It literally means that they believed on Him, but He did not believe on them.

Do you know that there is a faith that leads to Hell? It is a false faith; a counterfeit faith; a temporary faith. It is not a faith which desires to be changed to be like Christ. It is a faith which says, "I just want the blessings." It is a faith that believes in miracles but does not believe the Word of God by obeying it.

BUT there is a true faith that says, "Give me Jesus! I long for Him and I want to burn for Him!"

CHRIST THE ROCK

Paul, writes in Ephesians 2:19-22, *"Ye...are the household of God; And are built upon the foundation of the apostles and prophets, Jesus Christ himself being the chief corner stone; In whom all the building fitly framed together groweth unto an holy temple in the Lord: In whom ye also are builded together for an habitation of God through the Spirit."*

Peter also writes, *"Wherefore also it is contained in the scripture, Behold, I lay in Sion a chief corner stone, elect, precious: and he that believeth on him shall not be confounded"* (I Pet.2:6).

Isaiah writes, *"Therefore thus saith the Lord GOD, Behold, I lay in Zion for a foundation a stone, a tried stone, a precious corner stone, a sure foundation: he that believeth shall not make haste"* (Isa28:16).

If you believe in Christ the Rock; if you believe in Christ as your foundation, you will not be confounded; you will not be moved; you will not be confused. Your whole trust will be in Him. You can go through temptation, through trials, through horrible darkness; nights of confusion; through circumstances that you do not understand but because Christ is your rock and the cornerstone of your life, you will come through.

In Matthew 16:13-18, we read that Jesus asks His Disciples, *"Who say you that I am?"* and Peter being Peter, speaks first (of course Peter is always the first to get it right and always the first to get it wrong!) and says, *"Thou art the Christ"* and Christ goes on to tell Peter that, *"...flesh and blood have not revealed this unto thee but my Father which is in heaven..."* Then in verse 18, *"And I say also unto thee, That thou art **Peter** [petros], and upon this **rock** [petra] I will build my church; and the gates of hell shall not prevail against it"* (v18). The word *'petros'* means a piece of rock, but *'petra'* means a mass of rock. The Rock is Christ, revealed as the Son of God. But Peter is only a little rock or pebble. This is where the Catholic Church has gone wrong: they have built the whole church on *'petros'* rather than on *'petra';* Peter rather than Christ. I would not want to put my eternal salvation in Peter's hands. One minute he is saying he will die for Christ, the next minute he denies Him to a little girl. One minute he speaks by a revelation from the Father, the next he speaks words given by Satan. I would not want to be building on a foundation like Peter—that is a bad foundation. Yes, he saw revival; he was a great preacher and saw great things but Peter is a poor foundation. Christ was saying it is upon me, Christ, the rock that you are to be built and as a result the gates of Hell shall not prevail against you.

If you build your house, family or church on the revelation of WHO CHRIST IS, the person of Christ, then all Hell will not be able to destroy you; Hell will never triumph over you. It does not matter how weak you are; how vulnerable you feel; how much you feel you are about to fail, if you build on the WRITTEN Word and its revelation of Christ, that HE is the Rock, the foundation of your life, all Hell cannot knock you out of this church. It is impossible.

Matthew 7:17 says, *"Even so every good tree bringeth forth good fruit; but a corrupt tree bringeth forth evil fruit."* Many people in the Church make great mistakes when they ignore such verses. If someone brings forth evil fruit in their life, character, nature, lifestyle and in their conduct, then it does not matter what they say or do, or what they say they have experienced, they are not born-again.

Again Matthew 7:21 says, *"Not every one that saith unto me, Lord, Lord,* (they know He is LORD) *shall enter into the kingdom of heaven; but he that doeth the will of my Father which is in heaven. Many will say to me in that day, Lord, Lord, have we not prophesied in thy name? and in thy name have cast out devils? and in thy name done many wonderful works* (Holy Ghost works)?*"* Understand, these are Pentecostals or Charismatic folk; they are people who believe; they are operating in the things of the Spirit; prophesying, casting out demons and doing many wonderful *'dunamos'* works (Acts 1:8)—that is mighty Holy Ghost works. Yet Christ says, *"And then will I profess unto them, I never knew you* [Greek: I never at any time, or in any way, ever knew you, or had intimate contact with you] *depart from me, ye that work iniquity."* That word, *'knew,'* means intimate, personal knowledge in a genuine relationship. They may be moved upon of the Holy Spirit like Saul who then died in battle and went to Hell[1], yet Christ says, 'I never at all knew you or had a personal relationship with you, so depart from me you workers of iniquity.' The fruit was bad; the heart was bad; there was no foundation in the life. If, however, you make Christ your foundation you have nothing to fear!

---

[1] Although Saul, as first king of Israel, was chosen for the task by the Lord and anointed of the Holy Spirit, it was not long until he turned from being a humble and obedient servant to being a man filled with anger, jealousy, resentment, fear, suspicion, and one who turned to witchcraft. We are told in II Samuel 7:15, *"But my mercy shall not depart away from him, as I took it from Saul, whom I put away before thee."* In this scripture the Lord is comparing Saul to the son of David, Solomon. He says in the previous verse, *"If he commit iniquity, I will chasten him with the rod of men, and with the stripes of the children of men"* but He was not going to take away His mercy from Solomon as He took it from Saul. He took His mercy from Saul and put him away from before Him. When David laments over his death he says that Saul's shield was cast away, *"as though he had not been anointed with oil"* (II Sam.1:21). There can be no doubt that Saul died in a lost, tormented state even though he had genuine dealings of God and genuine experiences of the Spirit.

I Cor.3:10-11, *"According to the grace of God which is given unto me, as a wise masterbuilder, I have laid the foundation, and another buildeth thereon. But let every man take heed how he buildeth thereupon. For other foundation can no man lay than that is laid, which is Jesus Christ."* Then Matthew 24, *"Therefore whosoever heareth these sayings of mine, and doeth them,* [note: not just hearing but obeying] *I will liken him unto a wise man, which built his house upon a rock: And the rain descended, and the floods came, and the winds blew, and beat upon that house; and it fell not: for it was founded upon a rock. And every one that heareth these sayings of mine, and doeth them not, shall be likened unto a foolish man, which built his house upon the sand: And the rain descended, and the floods came, and the winds blew, and beat upon that house; and it fell: and great was the fall of it."* It is not enough to receive the Word of God with initial great joy. That is not sufficient. **The Word of God must produce a life that is changed**. These two men are both so-called Disciples of Christ. Both were hearing the Word of God and listening; both want to go to meetings and conferences and both sit there and listen but their foundations are different as determined by their OBEDIENCE to the Word of God. Both have been enlightened but only one lives out the Word they have heard.

A fool knows everything but he does nothing. That is the man in that cage. He is a worker of iniquity; he does not have a changed life; in reality he believes nothing. Paul wants these Hebrews to go on to perfection which is why he warns them of the man in the iron cage. Christ, in talking about the wise and foolish man, is warning us of building on the sand. That foolish man did build a nice house—a nice Christian life—and it would have been fine for a while until the floods and winds came. That flood is the flood of iniquity which took that house down because the foundation was not Christ. That house could not stand in the day of God's judgment and would not keep them until Eternity or get them into Heaven.

Remember, Judas knew everything. Judas kissed Heaven but went to Hell. Judas kissed the cheek of Heaven itself, of the very one who was going to bleed and die on a Cross. Judas saw all the miracles, was chosen to be an Apostle, had a gifted

22

ministry, was sent out to preach, and even fooled the demons of Hell if he was used to cast them out. Even the demons of Hell could not see through Judas at that stage. Judas sold Christ for 30 pieces of silver because Christ was not his foundation. He had tasted Christ and was illuminated by the Word; he enjoyed them for a time and was excited; he could talk about experiences and he could say that Christ had called him, but he did not really care about Christ.

But the wise man obeys God and builds upon the Rock, Christ Jesus, and the floods and winds will never knock that house down. *"Nevertheless the foundation of God standeth sure, having this seal, The Lord knoweth them that are his. And, Let every one that nameth the name of Christ depart from iniquity"* (II Tim.2:19). That word *seal* is a beautiful word. It means a mark of ownership; to be **fenced-in in order to protect from misappropriation**; to have the impress of a stamp; a **mark of privacy or genuineness.** It is God's foundation. Paul is saying that we know that it is Christ's foundation because there is a *seal* on it; a seal like the wax seal that was used in ancient days to put on a scroll or letter to show from whom the letter had come and to make sure that the letter was not broken open between its source and its destination. Such a seal put a guard on that letter so that when you received it you knew who it was from and that no one else had opened it. Where this true foundations is found, you find God's seal saying, 'This is mine! I am going to protect anyone who builds on this foundation or teaching. Those who believe on me and obey me, are the real converts.'

This is what it is to be a Christian. You have built on repentance. You have built on faith. You have been baptized in water; you believe in the judgment of God. Well, God says, 'I am putting my seal on them to say that they are real Christians.' *"The Lord knoweth them that are his. And, Let every one that nameth the name of Christ depart from iniquity."* **If you want to prove to me that you are a Christian, do not just tell me your testimony** (although I love hearing testimonies), **do not just raise your hands in the meeting on Sunday—depart from iniquity!** When Christ is our foundation we will flee and run from iniquity; hating those things that used to dominate our life.

We all know Peter failed, David failed; we know great men

23

who really blew it, but they dusted themselves off, like the righteous man who falls seven times and gets up in order to pursue again after Christ once more. In getting up and continuing on, he proves that he is a real believer; a real convert (Prov.24:16).

CHAPTER 2

FOUNDATION OF REPENTANCE

Hebrews 6:1–2 *"Therefore leaving the principles of the doctrine of Christ, let us go on unto perfection; not laying again the foundation of **repentance** from dead works, and of faith toward God, of the doctrine of baptisms, and of laying on of hands, and of resurrection of the dead, and of eternal judgment."*

To stand in time and Eternity we must have a sure foundation. We are dealing with Eternity. We must give earnest heed and deep consideration to these foundations, for depending on these foundations we will either stand in Eternity or perish in Eternity. Too many people have sat in churches but are now out in the world because they did not give heed to these foundations. Do not take these for granted. We must be sure concerning our foundations of faith.

The very angels, seeing the wheat and the tares (the real converts and the false converts; those who really know Christ and the hypocrites) growing together as if they are exactly the same are so shocked and disturbed by this confusion that they ask the Lord if they can go in and separate them, but the Lord says, 'No, let them grow until the day of harvest when the weeds will be burnt up.' The reason being that in pulling up the tares the wheat would be pulled up as well. God tells them to leave them until the time of harvest (Mt.13:24-30).

Wheat and tares (weeds) look the same outwardly, but will look different after a storm and at harvest time. It has been said that the true wheat drops its head but the tares continue to stand upright at harvest time. At that time, the wheat will be more evident and the tares will be burnt. Also after a storm, wheat can look very battered and bowed over, but weeds will remain standing upright. In the church tares can seem at times to come through storms better than the true wheat.

The Bible also says that the Angels of Heaven rejoice over

one sinner who truly repents. Angels get frustrated over the counterfeit but just one sinner who truly repents causes the angels of Heaven to praise and worship. Please notice it does not say, 'one sinner who truly *believes*' it says *"one sinner that repenteth."* The Angels look for repentance and rejoice when they see it (Lk.15:10).

Hebrews 6:1-9 *"Therefore leaving the principles of the doctrine of Christ, let us go on unto perfection; not laying again the foundation of **repentance from dead works**, and of faith toward God, Of the doctrine of baptisms, and of laying on of hands, and of resurrection of the dead, and of eternal judgment. And this will we do, if God permit. For it is impossible for those who were once enlightened, and have tasted of the heavenly gift, and were made partakers of the Holy Ghost, And have tasted the good word of God, and the powers of the world to come, If they shall fall away, to renew them again unto repentance; seeing they crucify to themselves the Son of God afresh, and put him to an open shame. For the earth which drinketh in the rain that cometh oft upon it, and bringeth forth herbs meet for them by whom it is dressed, receiveth blessing from God: But that which beareth thorns and briers is rejected, and is nigh unto cursing; whose end is to be burned. But, beloved, we are persuaded better things of you, and things that accompany salvation, though we thus speak."*

I am persuaded that we are a real church: a born-again church that has been birthed of God; that we fellowship together as real believers and that we have real repentance in our midst but like Paul we have to deal with things—serious things.

Paul writing in verse 1: *"Therefore leaving the principles of the doctrine of Christ, let us go on unto perfection; not laying again..."* That word *leaving* means to move on, to move beyond, or to build upon. He is saying that we are going to move on by building upon these six fundamental doctrines. We should not stay at foundation level; we are going to leave them and move on. If we are weak at repentance, then we will not go on into the deeper things of God. We must have a solid foundation so that we can be sure to **move on**.

Once the foundation is laid, we must then leave it and move on: *let us go on*, which means to be carried along, to drive forward, or to be driven forward unto *perfection* which means completion or full maturity. On one hand it is our responsibility that we do not stay in immaturity; we must move on. But on the other hand, we are 'carried along' by God who stirs us up through the preaching of His Word, through our gathering together in fellowship and through conviction of sin. This desire to move on should burn in us: "I do not want to stay carnal. I do not want to stay immature. I do not want year after year to be facing the same issues that come up in my heart." **To go forward is a vital part of the call of the Gospel.**

So Paul is saying that once we have laid that foundation we can be carried on or driven forward by God. Christ does not want us to stay as a baby or child, or as an infant. He does not want you to remain carnal. He wants us to go on to maturity in Christ. Your heart ought to burn with that desire to be changed to be like Christ. We need to stir up that desire.

Just as a parent expects a child to grow up, get married and get a home, so Christ expects us to grow and mature. We will not fulfil the purpose and plan of God unless these vital foundations are in place and very solid. Many people do not grow in Christ and deal with issues in their life because these foundations are not laid in correctly.

Everybody says, "I know about repentance. I know about faith..." But why is there no real repentance in many lives? Repentance should be evident by change in your life. **It is not enough to mentally know these things—it must affect us in a real way and change our view of life.**

"...not laying again the foundation of repentance from dead works, and of faith toward God." Paul is showing us that we should not 'keep going back'; we need to move on. Repentance, faith, baptism in the Holy Ghost...that is not all there is, and these are not our goal. Rather it is from these foundations that we must move on to perfection. If these six foundational doctrines are there, we might say, "I'm on my way to Heaven," but that is not the point. A foundation was laid for a purpose and if you are just happy to be on your way to Heaven, then you have missed God's purpose for your life. **Our goal is perfection.** *"...not laying again,"* means not building anew or once more: The foundation is absolutely vital but it is not the goal; the goal is

perfection. Without building on the foundation the foundation loses its purpose.

In Hebrews chapter three, we read of Israel, millions of people, walking through the Wilderness. For 10 days they walked through the Wilderness. God had made a promise that He was going to give them a land; a Land flowing with milk and honey; a land of great blessing; a land of great victory. The Promised Land is a picture of a victorious life in Christ but we are told that **through their unbelief**, God said, *"I sware in my wrath, They shall not enter into my rest"* (3:11). He made a solemn unbreakable pledge that that generation would not enter the land and that they would die in the Wilderness.

The Bible says that God made a *"...breach of promise"* (Num 14:34). God made a generation gap and basically said, 'They will not fulfil my will and purpose on earth. Oh yes, they will get to Heaven. I will walk in their midst and do miracles. I will provide for them and answer their prayers. I will protect them and do many things for them but that generation will never fulfil my purpose.' So for forty years God leaves them wandering in a wilderness because of their unbelief. They were not interested in fulfilling the plan and purpose of God. Christians can be like that walking for years seeing the same situations in their lives, the same characteristics, the same attitudes, not willing to deal with issues. They are happy to just know God and be on their way to Heaven. But God has given us a solid foundation in order that we might raise up a building for His glory, for His indwelling.

These six doctrines are like three coins, with two sides on each coin and these three coins go together. There is no contradiction in anyone of them. They join together in perfect unity.

- On the first coin you have real repentance on one side and real faith on the other side.
- On the second coin we have the doctrine of Baptisms and on the reverse side we have Laying on of Hands.
- On the third coin we have Eternal Judgement with Resurrection of the dead on the other side.

You may ask, "How do I get faith?" Don't worry about 'getting faith' if you truly repent, faith will follow. True repentance always precedes faith and is always followed by true faith. Sinners say, "I don't have enough faith to believe in God..." but faith is not the issue. If we preach repentance and a sinner *truly repents*, faith will follow. God will give the gift of faith. Sinners may say, "I'm not sure about Noah's Ark, about all those miracles. I'm not sure I can believe that God created all things..." If they try to grasp all of that before they come to Christ, they may end up nowhere, but **faith to believe that the Bible is true will follow true, genuine repentance**. God will give them that supernatural faith when they repent of their sins.

Repentance is the first foundation and therefore should have priority. If you have not repented, you have simply not been born-again. *"...repent and believe..."* (Mt.4:17; Mk.1:15). The message of the Gospel is *Repent and Believe*—not just believe, but first repent then believe.

In the New Testament they never preached 'believe in God' without first preaching repentance. Likewise, when we witness to friends, family, or strangers we should preach repentance. We are inclined to say, "Just believe in God," but we must tell them to repent. In their hearts they cannot believe because they do not have the ability because they have not repented. We should tell them to TURN AWAY FROM their sin; be convicted of their sin and God will give them faith.

Again Paul was, *"Testifying both to the Jews, and also to the Greeks, repentance toward God, and faith toward our Lord Jesus Christ"* (Acts 20:21). Both to the Jews and to the Gentiles, Paul made it his priority to preach repentance then he preached faith toward God. All Hell cannot shake the faith which follows repentance.

HOW REPENTANCE IS DEALT WITH IN THE NEW TESTAMENT

John the Baptist's first message was repentance. The beginning of his ministry was marked by an emphasis upon repentance: *"Repent ye: for the kingdom heaven is at hand"* (Mt.3:2). This was equivalent to saying the kingdom of God was at hand. By saying that the *'kingdom of heaven is at hand'* John was saying 'Heaven is so real; the things of God are so real; Eternity is so real that you could reach out and touch it. The realm of Christ's reign is within reach. We are on the very edge of the Kingdom of God being made manifest, so repent; get your lives right. Do not delay.' When preaching loses the message of repentance preaching is finished. **True preaching always begins with repentance and continues with repentance**. Mark 1:4, *"...preach the baptism of repentance for the remission of sins."* Without repentance there is no remission, or forgiveness of sins.

Repentance is the avenue, the entrance and the pathway to total forgiveness. It is the only way to all your sins being cancelled, all your guilt being removed, all your condemnation being relinquished and of delivering you from an eternity in Hell. When a man or woman experiences true repentance, all their sins are forgiven. Trying to believe that all your sins are forgiven is not the issue. Forgiveness comes on the back of true repentance. Without true repentance—when a man turns from his sin and truly repents from his heart—there is no forgiveness; he will still be condemned and guilty without repentance. True repentance will always drive you to Christ, drive you to the blood, drive you to the Cross and drive you to forgiveness.

People come to meetings and they say, "I want to be forgiven. I want to be free from my sins. Pray for me to be free." But without repentance they cannot get free. **If you want to be free from condemnation you must repent.** Repentance is the pathway to all forgiveness and to being set free. All your sins are forgiven on the back of repentance. Repentance is powerful. Repentance liberates us. Repentance brings us to the cleansing blood, the Cross and Christ. There is no point in saying, "Do you want all your sins forgiven? Then just believe in God." That is half a Gospel. The issue is WILL THEY REPENT? There is no point in preaching freedom from sin if you do not preach repentance.

John came preaching the Baptism of Repentance and it marked his whole ministry. An older lovely, godly woman once said to me, "I don't like Leonard Ravenhill's preaching very much. He's a bit negative isn't he?" I replied, "Well, no not really. I enjoy his preaching. John the Baptist's preaching might have sounded different from Paul's preaching but everything that

John said about Christ was true; it was real. You could have gone down to the river Jordan and heard John preaching, yelling, shouting, and frothing at the mouth; and he was preaching repentance. People might have said, 'Does John not have another message? I went Monday and he was preaching repentance. I went Tuesday and he was preaching repentance. I went Wednesday, Thursday and Friday and he was preaching repentance. Doesn't he have any other message?'"

For six months John preached repentance until they killed him because he preached against sin. **Do not grow weary of hearing the message of repentance.** Repentance was the message given to John by God. He was consumed with repentance because he knew that he was making a way for the Lamb of God who was going to wash away their sins. He knew he was making a way for the Baptizer in the Holy Ghost. He knew that repentance was preparing the hearts and making the people ready for the living God. His whole vision, goal, and dream was to make ready a people. In order for the people to be prepared to receive the Gospel, repentance had to be preached. Repentance prepares the heart; prepares the mind; prepares the life for God. Without repentance you cannot meet God face to face. You cannot have God draw near you unless you have repented. It would be a fearful and terrible thing to draw near to God without repenting.

In Matthew 3:8, John preached, *"Bring forth therefore fruits meet for repentance:"* In other words, bring forth fruits that show me that you have repented. The men and women on the banks of the Jordan could not have just waded down to John in the water and said, "Baptize me, John, because I believe your message." That was not sufficient in itself. No, they had to bring forth fruits. They had to demonstrate that they had repented. John would have asked them to prove it by their lifestyle.

John said, "I am going to baptize you in water. I am looking at the outward. I am looking at you. I am listening to you but if you have really repented, when you leave here prove it in your life, prove it in your home and prove it over the next six months." *By their fruit you shall know them.* John knew that if a man or woman had truly repented in their heart then everyone who knew them would soon see it. Somebody who has repented

31

does not carry on in the same old life and habits. **A radical change comes with repentance**. We can look at someone and know that something has happened to them. When people in the world see the change in you they may not understand it but they will notice a change. They may not like it but they will acknowledge it. That is 'fruit meet for repentance.'

Again, a man can come forward at an altar call and cry, but if he has not repented in his heart we will not see a change. When someone professes a change, I go looking for that fruit after six months or a year down the road. That is simply wise.

John the Baptist, said, *"And now also the axe is laid unto the root of the trees: therefore every tree which bringeth not forth good fruit is hewn down, and cast into the fire"* (Mt.3:10). The Axe is the symbol of repentance, just like the Cross is the symbol of Christ's work on the Cross or the dove the symbol of the Holy Spirit. The Holy Ghost came down **as** a dove—not a literal dove—that was the only way he could describe it. In the very same way repentance is described or symbolized as an axe. An axe is for cutting down trees.

Some time ago I asked my wife to go to the hardware store and buy me an axe so that I could cut down some trees. Upon her return however, she handed me a hatchet. I told her that what she had purchased was not an axe and I described to her what an axe was; that it was about treble the length of the hatchet she had bought and that the hatchet was just for lopping off branches, whereas the bigger instrument, the axe, would enable me to chop down trees. This was news to her as through the years she had called a hatchet an axe and an axe a hatchet. This has happened with the word **repentance** in many churches today. We are confused over the word repentance. We think it is alright just to say, "Oh Lord, I'm sorry, just forgive me," but then to carry on living the same way. God will ask, "What is that? It is not true repentance." My wife soon learnt that an axe and a hatchet are similar but they are not the same. A hatchet is a smaller version of an axe but useless for the task I had in mind. A hatchet cannot do what an axe can do!

John says, *"...now also the axe is laid unto the root of the trees: therefore every tree which bringeth not forth good fruit is hewn down, and cast into the fire"* (Mt.3:10-11). If we do not experience the axe of repentance, we will experience the axe of God's judgment cutting us down and taking us to Hell. **Repentance is a violent thing.** Repentance is an issue of zeal; if you want to repent over your sin or an issue in your heart or an issue in your mind and you know that God commands you to repent, then REPENT!

A man or woman must say, "I have had enough of anger in my life." Or, "I have had enough of gossip in my life." Or, "I have had enough of unforgiveness in my life." Or "I have had enough of lust or jealousy in my life." Whatever the re-occurring issue is in your life of which you have said, "I have had enough!" If it keeps coming back, the man must take an axe to that issue. It must be torn down, not pruned.

The contemporary Church ministries of counselling and 'Inner Healing'—which is nothing else than secular psychology—just prunes a branch or plucks off a leaf, but the true message of repentance lays an axe to the root and brings the whole tree down.

We must keep the blade of our axe sharp and we need to keep it with us at all times so that when something starts to come up in on our heart, we can lay the **axe of repentance** to the root. We must not tolerate that attitude or thing in our heart, life, or mind. The axe of repentance is an act without sympathy.

Again, if we do not repent like that, then God will take an axe and by His judgment take us down to Hell.

Jesus Christ began His preaching ministry with the word and teaching of repentance. Matthew 4:17, *"Jesus began to preach, and to say, Repent: for the kingdom of heaven is at hand."* When you begin with something you carry on with it. It does not just say that He began with it and left it. He continued with this message throughout His ministry on Earth and left us with this message. Jesus never stopped preaching repentance. Throughout His whole ministry He preached repentance which is why they crucified Him.

This was Christ's last message and commission on Earth after His death and resurrection, *"And that **repentance and remission** of sins should be preached in his name among all nations, beginning at Jerusalem"* (Lk.24:47). He is saying, preach repentance in Jerusalem, preach it in Judea, preach it in

Samaria, preach it in the city of Rome, preach it out across the Roman Empire—preach repentance and remission of sins everywhere. Again, before you preach remission—concerning God forgiving your sins—or about grace, or about God loving you, preach repentance. This was Christ's last instruction to the Church and He has not changed His orders. He does not give us permission to tone down the preaching or just speak about forgiveness. Oh no! He said to His church, 'Everywhere you go preach repentance.' Some say, "Ah, but the Muslim doesn't need to hear repentance. The English don't need to hear repentance. Cultures are different. Repentance is an old-fashioned message; it's not contemporary. Just preach the love of God..." Oh yes, **the message of *repentance* may be old-fashioned, but it is for every soul, irrespective of religion, culture or generation.**

Christ's LAST MESSAGE was repentance. In Revelation 3:19, in speaking to the Church at Laodicea He said, *"As many as I love, I rebuke and chasten: be zealous therefore, and repent."* Even from Heaven, Christ was preaching repentance to the Church. NOTE: **to the Church** Christ was preaching repentance—not just to the sinner, not just to the man wanting forgiveness, but to the church of Laodicea. This church was birthed about 40 years prior to Christ bringing this message of repentance to them. It was a church birthed in revival. When Paul first went to Ephesus and preached the Gospel from 54 AD to 57 AD a mighty revival broke out that reached into all of Asia affecting every community. As a result a church was planted in Laodicea. They were deeply impacted by genuine apostolic ministry and revival. They sat under true preaching and teaching from genuine men of God, yet 40 years down the road Christ is preaching repentance to them because they had become lukewarm and backslidden.

Christ calls five of the seven churches of Asia to repentance (mentioned six times). Only 40 years after the beginning of those seven churches, Christ brings the message of repentance to five of them. Those five are told of the consequences of not repenting. e.g.: *'if you do not repent I will remove the candlestick...if you do not repent I will come against you, hate you and fight against you...if you do not repent I will cast you into great tribulation...if you do not repent I will come as a thief in the night when you will not expect me to come...'* These are all 'church people' who say they have known these things for many years. There was something wrong with the foundation of five of these seven churches. Though birthed as a consequence of apostolic ministry in Ephesus, five were lacking repentance in their foundation. Repentance was not an up-to-date condition of their heart and the spiritual consequence was terrible. Christ then had to tell them to come back to this foundation of repentance. Wrong doctrine, wrong attitudes, wrong lifestyle, and wrong order in the church had come in, so Christ told them to repent. **The only way back to God's order and the only way to true revival is by the way of repentance**. The Church of today *does* need to hear a message of repentance.

Only two churches were not told to repent; these were Philadelphia and Smyrna. The name of the first, Philadelphia, means "brotherly love", because they were filled with the love of God. They loved the Word, they loved Christ, they loved one another, and they loved holiness. Because they were the faithful, brotherly-love church, God did not need to call them to repentance. They were walking in the love of Jesus Christ and they were not called to repent.

The second church, Smyrna, was a small persecuted church. In this condition of opposition they stayed close to the Lord and kept their hearts right with Him and each other. Many churches in our world today that are under persecution are pure churches. The persecution keeps them heavily dependent upon the Lord; as a result they are preserved holy with their eyes on Christ alone. When we look at China we know that generally speaking it is a pure church and that it has experienced dramatic growth in the midst of the persecution.

The Early Church: The day of Pentecost was a miraculous, supernatural act of God but somebody still had to get up and preach repentance. Peter's first message on that day, in the midst of revival and after the crowd had cried out, *"What must we do?"* was, *"**Repent, and be baptized** every one of you in the name of Jesus Christ for the remission of sins, and ye shall receive the gift of the Holy Ghost"* (Acts 2:38).

Miracles are not enough. Supernatural tongues or manifestations are not enough—repentance must be preached.

When revival comes we must continue to preach and teach repentance. **Some revivals of history made the mistake that once God had come in power, they ceased to preach and teach as they used to and this is a great danger.** We must preach more *in* revival than we do before revival. So Peter said, 'If you want to receive the supernatural gift of the Holy Ghost then you must repent.'

Peter continued to preach repentance. *"Repent ye therefore, and be converted, that your sins may be blotted out..."* (Acts 3:19). Not only do we see him preaching repentance in the midst of revival on the day of Pentecost but also in the period following he continued to preach a pointed message of repentance. 'If you want your sins blotted out you must repent; if you want to be converted, repent.' Repentance is the first foundation and Peter knew it.

Do you know that this was Simon the Sorcerer's problem? He wanted to buy the gift of the Holy Ghost but Peter discerned that he had never truly repented and been born-again. Peter told him that his issue was repentance. Peter told Simon, 'Your money perish with you, Simon—you are still in the bond of iniquity...' (Acts 8:23). Simon believed—oh yes, he believed— but he had not repented. This is not a saving faith. You can have an intellectual faith; you can have an emotional faith but you can still lack a *true* saving faith. Simon the Sorcerer had never repented of his old heart attitudes which he had operated in as a sorcerer in Samaria. He kept all his wicked heart motivations intact and brought them into the church when he joined it. We are indeed told that *"Simon himself believed also...and was baptized"* (Acts 8:13) yet this was not saving faith. This was an intellectual or emotional faith but was not accompanied by a heart change. It was a faith without repentance. He continued to operate with the same heart but now under a religious veneer.

Peter said to Simon the Sorcerer, *"Repent therefore of this thy wickedness..."* (Acts 8:22). Peter is clear in telling Simon that he has never repented or dealt with his heart. Simon believed what he had heard and was caught up in this community changing revival; he wanted to go to Heaven and he had been baptized in water; but Peter knew by the Spirit of God and the confirmation of Simon's own lips that his great need was heart repentance. He had never repented. Wickedness still controlled his thoughts, his emotions, his feelings but it was covered in a religious veneer. We must destroy wickedness through repentance—that is the only cure. And so we see that Peter continued to preach the message of repentance.

Then Paul, as he looks back over 20 years of ministry says that he, "...*shewed first unto them of Damascus, and at Jerusalem, and throughout all the coasts of Judaea, and then to the Gentiles, that they should repent and turn to God, and do works meet for repentance"* (Acts 26:20). So in every region, community and in every church where Paul went in those first 20 years he preached repentance and looked for the fruits of repentance. He looked for a changed life that manifested fruit which revealed genuine heart repentance. He looked for them to bring forth works that reflected such repentance.

So, John the Baptist, Christ and the Early Church all preached repentance.

Now, the medium for repentance coming to hearts is usually through preaching. In the Church today they dumb-down preaching and replace it with mimes, funny acts, new strategies, and methodologies. All these things replace preaching or at least squeeze it into a corner. They attempt to justify such actions with the argument that 'we are not changing the message but just the method', but they are terribly wrong. God has ordained the preaching of the Gospel and if we change anything, God will be offended. God has ordained that this message of repentance come to sinners and to saints through the method of preaching, and if you change that, it will not have the same effect.

We so easily lose the meaning of words like repentance. **Repentance is not penitence.** The Catholic Bible (the Douay-Rheims) replaces the word *repent* with *penance* but there is a big difference between penance and repentance. Penance means you can do something to merit forgiveness or by some act you can 'pay' for what you have thought or done. With penance there is no need for a change of mind, heart, or action. Penance requires you do something for past sins; repentance demands that you change. Penance will not give power over sin. **True repentance however, will change the mind, the heart, the actions, and the whole direction of life.** No priest can grant forgiveness.

37

Forgiveness only comes after true repentance.

This approach is not only found in Catholicism. In Evangelical circles we hear preaching which says, "Come and believe in Christ," and we see people lift their hands in this kind of Gospel appeal. They are then told that they are forgiven yet they continue to live in sin. Of course there can be genuine repentance in the individual's heart on an occasion such as this but many have not repented and then wonder why they have no power over sin. We have replaced repentance with mere momentary sorrow for sin and sadly even that is usually missing.

- **Christianity without repentance is no Christianity at all.**
- Repentance needs to be put back into the Evangelism.
- **We do not need to find a more contemporary or milder word than the good old-fashioned term 'repentance'.** It is a God-given word.

William Booth (1829-1912) said, "I consider that the chief dangers which confront the coming century will be religion without the Holy Ghost, Christianity without Christ, **forgiveness without repentance**, salvation without regeneration…and Heaven without an Eternal Hell." Mr. Booth was right: 'Just come and believe and God will forgive you,' is the half-message out there today. 'You don't need to change your attitude. You don't need to be broken over your sin. It doesn't matter how you live...' Mr. Booth was a prophet.

Acts 17:30, *"but now [God] commandeth all men every where to repent:"* **This is a command** of God. This is the New Covenant. This is the Grace and Love of God. **Because God loves us, He commands us to repent**. The message of repentance is an expression of the Love of God. Notice that it says *"all men every where."* That is very comprehensive. There is no exception for culture, age, colour, generation, or language.

WHAT DOES THE TERM 'REPENTANCE' MEAN?

The Hebrew:
i) *nacham, nocham* = a deep sigh; to regret one's actions regarding what one has done. So it is emotional; **something you feel** and experience.

ii) *shub* = to turn back; retreat or change direction. This is an action or **something you do**

Greek:
i) *metanoeo* (*metanoia*) = a change of mind; a reversal of the inward thought; to **think differently**; to reconsider. So if your mind has never changed then you have never repented.
ii) *metamellomai* = **to regret**; to care afterwards; to have deep concern.

We see that the Hebrew and Greek agree: **repentance is a deep grief and emotional regret (godly sorrow) for what you have done, as well as a change of thinking and direction of life.** Let us look at both elements of repentance more closely.

"Then Judas, which had betrayed him, when he saw that he was condemned, repented himself, and brought again the thirty pieces of silver to the chief priests and elders, Saying, I have sinned in that I have betrayed the innocent blood. And they said, What is that to us? see thou to that. And he cast down the pieces of silver in the temple, and departed, and went and hanged himself" (Mt.27:3-4).

Did Judas truly repent? NO! Yet the Bible says that when he saw what had happened, he 'repented himself' which is the Greek *metamellomai* meaning to regret, to care afterwards, or to have deep concern. Judas had an emotional repentance. He was sorry for the consequence of his sin but not sorry for his sin. In reality he was not sorry for his betrayal or his wickedness, but he had regret over what had happened. This emotional repentance even made him lose interest in the money and the house he had planned to build on the field, in which he ended up hanging himself.[2] So here is a man who has deep emotional regrets. Remember he was chosen to preach. He saw many a miracle and had many experiences with Christ but he was not clean. After the betrayal, Satan who had entered him left him 'high and dry'.

---

[2] Acts 1:20 says *"Let his habitation be desolate, and let no man dwell therein..."* This word *"habitation"* means a country house or cottage. After Judas' suicide it was to be left deserted. No one was to take up residence in it. From this it seems likely that Judas wanted the money, the 30 pieces of silver, in order to buy this land and property. His retirement plan! But in remorse he lost all interest and killed himself.

Typical of the Devil, he takes you on a journey then leaves you on your own with suicidal thoughts. Judas must have said, 'all for 30 stinking bits of silver...I don't care about it now. None of it means anything.' But even that terrible night of anguish through which Judas passed did not bring him to true repentance. **He did regret but he did not change the direction of his life.** Judas experienced deep emotion in terrible anguish, and regret, but did not change his mind or direction. Strong emotion alone is not evidence of repentance.

In Romans 9:13, Paul quotes the written Word, that God loved Jacob but hated Esau. Some try to say that God hated Esau before he sold his birthright and that God loved Jacob before he did any good. This has confused people who ask, "How could God say that He loved one man and hated another before they were born?" But not until Malachi are we told that God hated Esau. God did not say that he hated Esau until **after** Esau's sin and after his death. It was his own sinful heart that got him in trouble with God.

But Paul goes further. *"Lest there be any fornicator, or profane person, as Esau, who for one morsel of meat sold his birthright"* (Heb.12:16). We know that Esau, a cunning hunter and a man of the field, came in from the field at the point of fainting, feeling like he would die. In this state and condition he smelt the stew which Jacob was preparing and in order to obtain it, he sold his birthright (Heb.12:16-17; Gen.25:27-34). Esau was a sensual man: a man of the flesh who lived by his five senses. He was a man who lived by what he saw and what he heard. He was more interested in satisfying present need than thinking of future inheritance. He lived for the present, whereas Jacob lived for that which was of eternal consequence. Esau is a type of the carnal man whom we see so often in churches today who will sacrifice spiritual things to satisfy his belly in seeking after natural things. *"For ye know how that **afterward**, when he would have inherited the blessing, he was rejected: for he found no place of repentance, though he sought it carefully with tears"*(Heb 12:17). Please note that it was **afterward** that Esau started to think about what he had done—after he had satisfied his belly. After he had sold his birthright he changed his mind which is what this word **repentance** means here. Esau changed his mind but it was too late. You may have a change of mind but that is not true repentance.

There was no shortage of tears and emotion with Esau as he decided to change his mind, but it was too late. Again, as with Judas, he was not crying over his sin or his offence of a holy God; he was crying over the loss of his inheritance. His tears were selfish, self-centred and focused on time, not Eternity. Just like the *man in the Iron Cage* (*Pilgrims' Progress,* and Hebrews 6) it was impossible for Esau to be renewed which is why we must not take these things lightly. We cannot afford to play spiritual games. Esau went looking for his inheritance but he could not find it.

HOW CAN WE RECOGNIZE TRUE REPENTANCE?

There are three vital areas of man that repentance must affect: **the mind, the emotions, and the will.** In our mind or intellect there will be an intellectual change; we will think differently. In our emotions we will feel regret, grief, weeping, or sorrow. In our will we will make different decisions or choices. **If these three realms are not all touched then we have not repented.**

The perfect example of REAL REPENTANCE is the Prodigal Son (Lk.15:17-19):

1. He **changed his mind;** his thinking: *"he came to himself."* He was saying 'What have I done?'
2. He thought about the goodness of his Father's house. 'They have plenty, I have nothing.'
3. He recognised his **great need:** *"I perish with hunger!"* 'I am going to perish in my sin.'
4. There was an **inward change.** He said in his heart: *"I will arise and go to my father."* Our motives inwardly must be changed. An inward change is marked by the changing of the will, the making of a choice and a definite decision.
5. He **owned his personal guilt** and took responsibility for his actions: *"I have sinned against heaven, and before thee."*

6. He knew **shame** over his sin: *"...I am no more worthy to be called thy son."*
7. He **took action**: *"he arose, and came to his father."* He made a decision that led to this outward action. First an inward decision, then an outward action. An inward act of repentance that is not followed by this outward return is not true repentance. The absence of this 'outward action' (fruit) means that a decision had never truly been made.

It is not enough to confess your sin **you must forsake** your sin. *"He that covereth his sins shall not prosper: but whoso confesseth and forsaketh them shall have mercy"* (Prov.28:13). There has to be this outward act of forsaking sin to prove that heart repentance has taken place.

Eight marks of True Repentance:
The nature and fruit of true repentance

1. **Godly sorrow** (II Cor.7:10; Ps.38; Ps.18)—not just sadness for sin.
2. **Desire for forgiveness** (Lk.18:13) just like the Prodigal.
3. **Confession of sins** (Prov.28:13; Neh.9:2)—we cannot just say, "IF I have sinned against you, forgive me..." It must be specific.
4. **Shame for sin** (Eze.43:10; 20:43): grief at what you have done.
5. **Hatred for sin** (Eze.36:31; Ps.119:104): that which you once loved now you hate.
6. **Forsaking of sin** which is a turning from sin (Isa.55:7; Eze.14:6). Until you turn from sin, you have not repented.
7. **Turning to God** (I Thess.1:9; Zech.1:3). A consciousness of your sin will drive you to God. True repentance will always result in restored relationship and fellowship with God.
8. **Restitution** (Lk.19:8) like Zacchaeus who gave half of what he had to the poor and paid 4 times that which he owed. The man who was known for covetousness gave

half of all he owned away! That is true repentance. When repentance comes to your heart you will want to put things right with people.

That prodigal son experienced real repentance in his emotions, his feelings, his mind and his will—in his whole being. Once he was with the pigs and about to eat their swill, but he was welcomed back into the father's house. When the father ran to meet the Prodigal son he did not mention what the son had done. He did not tell the son, "You need to sort yourself out," because the son was already truly repentant, humbled and broken, small in his own sight and knew he did not deserve anything. Repentance had already done its work! **True repentance will cause God the Father to run toward the repentant sinner**. True repentance will put the best robe on your back, a ring on your finger, and shoes on your feet. Repentance lays a merry feast before you (v22-24). Repentance is not a negative thing—it is the key to every spiritual blessing.

As we come to the end of this chapter on Repentance, I want you to know that the Scriptures are clear in stating that repentance is a gift granted by God to sinners. **Repentance is the result of God's Grace at work in the heart of man**. Repentance is not a work; it is the result and fruit of Grace. Repentance comes before and leads to forgiveness, new life and the acknowledging of truth (Acts 5:31; 11:18; II Tim.2:25).

Repentance is one of the most wonderful and precious things we can experience from the hand of God and is the first foundation stone.

CHAPTER 3

FAITH TOWARD GOD

Heb.6:1-2 *"Therefore leaving the principles of the doctrine of Christ, let us go on unto perfection; not laying again the foundation of repentance from dead works, **and of faith toward God,** Of the doctrine of baptisms, and of laying on of hands, and of resurrection of the dead, and of eternal judgment. And this will we do, if God permit."*

And verses **9-11**: *"But, beloved, **we are persuaded** better things of you, and things that accompany salvation, though we thus speak. For God is not unrighteous to forget your work and labour of love, which ye have shewed toward his name, in that ye have ministered to the saints, and do minister. And we desire that every one of you do shew the same diligence to the full **assurance of hope unto the end.**"* The 'end' is that end of your Christian walk: the day when you meet Jesus Christ.

And verses **12-20,** *"That ye be not slothful, but followers of them who through faith and patience inherit the promises"* For when God made promise to Abraham, because he could swear by no greater, he sware by himself, Saying, Surely blessing I will bless thee, and multiplying I will multiply thee. And so, after he had patiently endured, he obtained the promise. For men verily swear by the greater: and an oath for confirmation is to them an end of all strife. Wherein God, willing more abundantly to shew unto the heirs of promise* [that's us] *the immutability* [un-changeability] *of his counsel, confirmed it by an oath That by two immutable things, in which it was impossible for God to lie, we might have a strong consolation* [encouragement] *, who have fled for refuge to lay hold upon the hope set before us: Which hope we have as an anchor of the soul, both sure and stedfast, and which entereth into that within the veil; Whither the* *forerunner is for us entered, even Jesus, made an high priest for ever after the order of Melchisedec."*

THE FOUNDATION OF FAITH

The six foundations of which we read in Hebrews chapter six, are called the *Foundations of Christ*. These are the basics; the elementary teachings for the Church and for the individual life. We have studied *Repentance* so the next foundation we must have in place is *faith toward God*. The five foundations following *Repentance* cannot be in place without that first and vital foundation of *Repentance*. Indeed, when *Repentance* is 'dumbed-down' there are grave consequences. When repentance is taken out of the Gospel and out of the lifestyle of believers, there are terrible consequences, **for faith cannot come without repentance**. Repentance and faith are connected. As illustrated in the previous chapter, they are two sides of the same coin. There is no contradiction—both are linked intimately—and you cannot separate them. Where you get real repentance you will get real faith; where you get real faith you will get real repentance.

Most of the problems we see across the Church today of worldliness, carnality and backsliding are all tragedies which come back to this: the lack of repentance. When repentance is undermined, there is a destruction of true faith.

The creation and promotion of ministries like *Inner Healing*, *Deliverance*, and *Christian Counselling* in our day is because Christ is not central any more. We have lost the simplicity of repentance—real, genuine life-changing repentance—and we have lost the reality of faith that comes out of repentance.

If you show me a man who says he believes in God but he has never repented, then you show me a liar. If you tell me of someone who says they have repented but they cannot believe in God, then you have shown me someone who has not really repented of their sins. **True repentance will drive us forward to true faith**. Anyone who has truly repented of their sin has been given faith in God. The Bible says, you did not seek God, but He came seeking you, which is why you suddenly became disturbed; that is why you had a desire to know God and why you suddenly became convicted of sin. That was not you but Christ because He loved you, and He died two thousand years ago for you.

Even when the most sceptical atheist repents of his sin, faith comes into his heart and he knows that God created all things. That faith came as a product of real repentance.

Show me a man who truly repents, who breaks over his sin, who feels his sin and turns from his sin, and you show me a man who walks by faith, who really knows what God-given faith is. Anyone who has side-stepped true repentance never has had true faith in God.

You cannot go on to have a genuine Baptism in the Holy Ghost without genuine Repentance. Neither is there any point or value at all (no good spiritually or eternally) in being baptized in water if you have not truly repented. Lack of repentance undermines every other biblical doctrine.

FAITH TOWARD GOD

This is not faith in faith; it is not faith in circumstances and it is not faith in the Church. It is *'faith toward God'* and it needs to be right in the roots of your Christian life. This faith is not focused on man, religion, or tradition; it is a faith utterly caught up in God.

Many people have 'a faith' which is not biblical faith. For example if you listen to the prosperity preachers or American television evangelists, they talk about having faith to get money or cars, or a house or physical possessions; having faith that God will bless you and give you everything. Now, there is an element of truth in those things but not the way they teach it. Their faith is more set on physical things than it is on God. The focus of their faith is not God. They could not say, "If I lose everything I am happy, because I have faith in God..." their faith uses God as a means unto physical attainment.

This issue of having *faith toward God* is absolutely foundational to your Christian walk. Your faith needs to be real and genuine in order that you can build upon it and walk by it. What can you possibly accomplish in the Christian life that is not 'by faith'?

Mark 1:15, *"...repent ye, and believe the gospel."* When you have faith toward God, you have faith toward the Gospel. The Gospel is, *repent and believe in Christ*; believe in the blood of Christ; put faith in the Word of God; this is true faith. This saving, foundational faith is a faith in the Gospel of Jesus Christ. This is not about strange, profound, or deep revelations about Christ and Melchisedec. This is basic faith: you are a sinner...do you believe that you are a sinner? That you were born a sinner? That you were on your way to Hell? Do you believe that Jesus Christ died on the Cross? Do you believe that He rose again on the third day? Do you believe that He is now ascended to the right hand of the Father? Do you believe that if you put your faith in Him you shall be saved from the wrath to come? This genuine saving faith is not faith in, or for physical things: it is a faith in what God says about Himself. It is faith in Jesus Christ.

"He that believeth and is baptized shall be saved; but he that believeth not shall be damned." (Mark 16:16) This verse shows me that baptism itself is not going to save us; it does not say *'he that is baptized shall not be damned"* but it says *"he that believeth not shall be damned."* You see, you can believe intellectually and be baptized, but not be saved. You can be baptized in water and yet still be damned. Baptism in water means nothing toward being saved; but real faith in Christ will save you from being damned eternally.

Every individual born physically is under the wrath of God. They are doomed unless they repent and believe. They will spend an eternity under the wrath of God in an eternal Hell if they do not repent and believe. That is what is weighing upon every single soul so unless this foundation of faith is laid-in, damnation is hanging above their head. Many people say they believe this but go out and live for themselves whilst damnation is still hanging above their head. They assure themselves by saying, "Oh, well, I believe that Jesus died for me..." but their life has not been transformed because they have never repented of their sin; they have never dealt with sin in their heart and never changed, but they are saying, "I believe Jesus died on the Cross. I believe there is a God. I believe there is salvation. I believe there is eternal life..." But they have never repented of their sin, so their faith is a dead faith. It is an intellectual faith.

They believe facts about Christ but it is not a faith that has turned them from sin unto righteousness.

PARABLE OF THE SOWER AND THE SEED:
Luke 8:4-15

Christ is the *Sower*, and the seed is the Word of God and as you know there are four different types of ground in this parable. So the *Sower* is the same; the seed is the same but the ground is different. The fruit produced from the seed depends upon the condition of the ground. The ground represents the hearts of men and women. The response to the Word of God will dictate what fruit comes out of a life.

Show me someone who brings forth little fruit or someone who brings forth great fruit and you reveal to me the state of their heart. The Word has a different effect on each heart because each heart is different. If your heart is in the right place, you will bring forth much fruit. But if your heart is not in the right place, you will not produce any fruit. It does not matter if the Word of God is expounded eloquently or if the preacher bursts a blood vessel in preaching, none of that makes a difference if the heart is not in the right place.

Note, what Christ says about one of these types of ground: **Luke 8:12**, *"Those by the way side are they that <u>hear</u>; then cometh the devil, and <u>taketh away the word out of their hearts</u>, lest they should <u>believe and be saved.</u>"*

Here are people who have heard the Word; are happy to receive it; they intellectually agree with the Word; they have no problem with the Word—they are not rejecting it, in fact it seems that they receive it into their heart, but they have not believed unto salvation. Again, they have received the seed of the Word that has the power to change their life yet they do not believe and therefore have not been saved. This shows us that you can have great dealings with the Word of God, the Lord can be speaking to you, yet if you never mix it with faith you will not come to real faith.

Here Jesus warns that the Devil comes to take away the Word because that Word has the potential to bring you to faith and to save you from your sin, from damnation and from Hell.

The Devil knows that the power is in the Word of God to change your life. It is all in the power of the Word of God so the Devil comes to steal the Word. The Devil is active in every life to contradict the Word of God. When you hear a convicting message, the Devil will come to you to steal that Word away from your understanding and out of your heart. We cannot just sit in meetings and carry on as if nothing opposes this Word. We are in a warfare for the Word of God. There is warfare over what you do with the Word of God. Hell knows the importance of the Word of God mixed with faith. Without the Word of God there is no faith. *"So then faith cometh by hearing, and hearing by the word of God."* (Romans 10:17) The Word of God and faith can never be separated.

Without the Word of God, what would we believe? We would not know what to believe! We would have no ground of confidence. The Word is settled in Heaven forever. The Word of God is perfect and cannot lie so we can rest our faith on that Word. We can believe it. When we take that seed of the Word and mix faith with it, it changes our life. We can sit in a meeting, hear one message and it can change the whole direction of our life. The Word can set us free from something, purely because it has caused faith to rise up in our heart. That is why it is not enough just to believe the Word in your head or just nod your head, or say, 'Amen', or say, 'Yes, I agree with that.' Do you actively mix faith with the Word of God? If you do not mix faith with the Word, the Word is of 'none effect'.

In Israel, in 1973, seeds were found within clay pots in the palace of King Herod the Great, at Masada. These seeds were from the Judean palm tree and had been extinct since at least 500 AD. The seeds were taken and planted in, 2005. By 2011, the palm tree was over two meters tall and had blossomed for the first time that year. For almost 2,000 years, the right mixture of elements—light, temperature, water, and oxygen—were missing. It was these very things that were needed in order to cause the seed to produce life. As a result the seed remained dormant for millennia. It is exactly the same with the seed of God's Word. The seed of the Word of God can seem to lie dormant for many years in the mind and life of a person. But suddenly it is brought out into the right environment and as a result breaks forth into abundant life. This happens when the Spirit of God moves on the seed in regeneration. The individual who mixes faith with that Word, will go on to raise up a godly testimony. A seed that once lay dormant now radically changes a life.

BY FAITH

"He that believeth on [into] *me hath everlasting life"* (John 6:47). *"For with the heart man believeth unto righteousness* [into righteousness—you believe into righteousness; faith literally moves you into a position of righteousness in Christ when you are truly born-again]; *and with the mouth confession is made unto salvation. For the scripture saith, Whosoever believeth on* [into] *him shall not be ashamed"* (Romans 10:10-11). Faith is a 'thing' of the heart; not the head.

This tells us that faith moves us. Faith will take us out of the kingdom of Satan and put us in to the kingdom of God. True faith will take away your sins. True faith will take you into a place of forgiveness. Faith moves you along. You cannot have true faith and remain the same or stay in the same place. True faith moves you into righteousness; into Christ. True faith took your life and put you into Christ. Faith is a moving word. It is not passive; it is not static. You show me someone who is really living by faith and you show me someone who is really growing in their walk with God. On the contrary, if someone goes to all the meetings and all the Conventions, yet never changes, I will show you someone with unbelief in their heart. They have no faith. The greatest preachers will not benefit them if they do not mix faith with the Word. But true faith takes you somewhere.

"For by grace are ye saved through faith; and that not of yourselves: it is the gift of God: Not of works, lest any man should boast."(Ephesians 2:8-9) **Through faith** you are born-again. Not by works. Faith is a gift—you cannot work faith up! Repentance is a gift. Faith is a gift. GOD grants repentance unto the heart of man. The Bible says that no man would come unto Him unless the Spirit of God drew him. No sinner has the desire to come of himself.

When we read Romans 4, we see the natural state of man in Adam, outside of Christ, where none is righteous; none is good;

none fears God; none seeks after God. Man outside of Christ does not even desire God.

If you meet a sinner and they say, "I seek God with all my heart," either they are a liar, or they are deceived, or the Spirit of God is working on them to move them toward the true Christ, because it is not natural to seek after Christ in a genuine real way. Anyone outside of Christ does not have a desire to seek after Him. It is the supernatural work of God to start drawing you and to give you repentance. Faith is the gift of God given to you when you truly repent. The only way to receive a true gift of faith is true repentance. You do not need to **try** and believe in God; you do not need to try and believe that God created the world, the moon, the stars, and the planets. No, God says, I am going to give you a faith that you may know that my Son hung on that Cross and bled and died for you 2,000 years ago. You are going to know that! You are going to know that I created all things 6,000 years ago. You are going to know that I have an eternal destiny for you. You are going to know all these things by a gift of genuine faith. You cannot believe these things naturally. You cannot grasp or understand them by your own power.

JUSTIFIED BY FAITH

Romans 5:1 *"Therefore being justified by faith, we have peace with God through our Lord Jesus Christ:"*
Galatians 2:16 *"Knowing that a man is not justified by the works of the law, but by the faith of Jesus Christ, even we have believed in Jesus Christ, that we might be justified by the faith of Christ, and not by the works of the law: for by the works of the law shall no flesh be justified"*
Galatians 3:24, *"Wherefore the law was our schoolmaster to bring us unto Christ, that we might be justified by faith."*
Romans 3:28, *"...justified by faith without the deeds of the law."*

The Catholic Church is built on faith **and** works. They say that it is both by grace *and* works that you are saved, but we know that we are *justified by faith alone.*

Martin Luther, nearly 500 years ago, stood up and declared

this Truth at the beginning of the Reformation: that it is by faith alone we are justified; by faith we are made righteous or made acceptable unto God...BY FAITH, not by works.

I want to warn you with great care: If ever you fail God; if ever you sin; if ever you fall short, do not think that you can work your way back! You cannot work your way back to being good enough or get back into a close place with God. You cannot strive toward that. What you have to do is stand still and simply believe. You are justified by faith. You are made righteous by faith. You are forgiven by faith. You are washed in the blood by faith. You are forgiven of your sins by faith. If ever you move to striving or trying to attain unto that sense of forgiveness by your works, efforts, or deeds, you will end up a very defeated, frustrated person. So many start with faith but carry on with works. To start in faith is something dynamic but if you carry on with self-effort or try to present something that you have accomplished to God, God will reject that; He only accepts faith.

True faith changes you. Show me true faith operating and I will show you a man that is walking by faith. **Justification by faith is foundational.** Faith is a gift given by the grace of God.

Romans 3:25 says we are to have, *"...faith in his blood..."* We are to have faith in the blood of Jesus which is not just a passive, intellectual understanding. It is that your heart literally believes that the blood was shed for you. We are to put our faith in the blood of Jesus. You do not need to understand how it works. All you need to know is that your faith is in the blood of the Lamb—that is all my salvation and all my redemption— knowing that you and I have nothing to offer God. I could walk with God for 50 years yet still not have anything of any consequence to offer God or commend me to Him.

- **Galatians 3:26** says, *"For ye are all the children of God by faith in Christ Jesus."* **You become a child of God by faith.**
- **Ephesians 3:17,** *"That Christ may dwell in your hearts by faith;"* **Christ dwells in your heart by faith.**
- **I Peter 1:5,** *"...kept by the power of God through faith..."* From the beginning unto the end of our walk with God we are kept through faith.

We live by faith; we walk by faith; we serve God by faith; we worship by faith. All is by faith.

We are told many times that *the just shall live by his faith:*

Habakkuk 2:4 *"Behold, his soul which is lifted up is not upright in him: but the just shall live by his faith."*

Romans 1:17 *"For therein is the righteousness of God revealed from faith to faith: as it is written, The just shall live by faith."*

Galatians 3:11 *"But that no man is justified by the law in the sight of God, it is evident: for, The just shall live by faith.*

Hebrews 10:38-39, *"Now the just shall **live** by faith: but if any man draw back, my soul shall have no pleasure in him. But we are not of them who draw back unto perdition; but of them that believe to the saving of the soul."*

Galatians 2:20, *"I am crucified with Christ: nevertheless I live; yet not I, but Christ liveth in me: and the life which I now live in the flesh I live by the faith of the Son of God, who loved me, and gave himself for me."*

When we speak in the natural about 'living' we mean everything you do: your breathing, your actions, and your conversation—the entirety of your life: everything you think, everything you say, everything you do. Now carry this over to living spiritually. You were washed in the blood by faith now you must 'live' your entire life by faith. Your prayer must be by faith; your service must be by faith; your worship must be by faith. ***Remember that without faith it is impossible to please God.***

God is not interested in our worship, evangelism, preaching, work, prayer, absolutely nothing, unless it flows out of a faith in Jesus Christ. When we witness, it must be by faith in Him; when I preach it must be by faith in the Son of God.

"...but if any man draw back, my soul shall have no pleasure in him..." God cannot be pleased with a life that is bankrupt of faith. There must be a living vital faith, not only in the foundation but all through your Christian walk. It must be a **living faith** which is alive unto God. A dead Christian is not a Christian at all. Someone who does not believe God's Word; that does not get stirred or inspired is dead and they do not realize it. A dead faith is no faith at all. An inactive faith is not biblical faith. If someone is not moving forward by faith, they are

drawing back from what God has said. But, thank God, there is a 'but'...

"...But we are not of them who draw back unto perdition; but of them that believe to the saving of the soul." Drawing back is unto destruction. Either you go forward in faith or you go back to destruction! These are the only choices. *"...them that believe to the saving of the soul..."* so there is a faith that will save your soul. Some believe for a time: they spring up, they believe and they say, "I am so happy to have found the Word of God and Christ." They receive it for a time but after a short time they fall away because they never believed unto the salvation of their soul. It was an intellectual faith; a short-term, temporary faith, but they really believed nothing.

THE DANGER OF UNBELIEF

Bear in mind that this letter was written to the Hebrew people less than a decade before the terrible destruction of Jerusalem in AD 70.[3] I am sure that many of them experienced Pentecost or at least the continuing influence of it as well as the teaching ministry of the apostles, yet Paul is warning them that they are in danger of drawing back; they are in danger of settling down into a half-way house; into a religious system; they are in danger of relying on the temple, the priesthood—in a dead religious system.

The Spirit of God who was inspiring this timely message to the Hebrew Christians was basically saying, 'In a few short years everything you hold dear will be gone. The temple, the city and priesthood will be no more. You must make sure that your faith and confidence is in Christ. You must go on to perfection in Christ.' So in Hebrews chapters 3 and 4, they are reminded of what happened to ancient Israel to keep them out of the Promised Land. It was **unbelief** that kept them out.

Hebrews 3:12 *"Take heed, brethren, lest there be in any of you*

---

[3] The Jewish nation today is a nation without forgiveness because there is no blood sacrifice being offered for them. Their own religion requires blood yet they no longer have such sacrifices. They ought to be crying out for the blood. Until then they have no salvation.

an evil heart of unbelief, in departing from the living God."
Hebrews 3:19 *"So we see that they could not enter in because of unbelief."*
Hebrews 4:6 *"Seeing therefore it remaineth that some must enter therein, and they to whom it was first preached entered not in because of unbelief."*
Hebrews 4:11 *"Let us labour therefore to enter into that rest, lest any man fall after the same example of unbelief."*

We must understand what the word unbelief means. The word for faith in Greek is *'pistia'* and the word for unbelief is *apistia*. The prefix 'a' literally means 'no', **so unbelief is 'no faith'** or is the exact opposite of having faith.

Paul uses the example of Israel's journey into the Promised Land as a very clear and serious warning to those in the church. He reminds them that God had sworn to give the land to Israel but they refused to believe Him. Paul warns that there are three stages of unbelief:

1. The first stage of unbelief is the **hardening of the heart.** *"Wherefore, as the Holy Ghost saith, Today if ye will hear his voice* [the Word of God], *Harden not your hearts, as in the provocation, in the day of temptation in the wilderness"* (Hebrews 3:7-8). The hearts of God's people were hardened through unbelief. Only 10 days out of Egypt and they had hardened their hearts. The hardening of the heart happens when the Holy Spirit is speaking to you but you refuse to listen. What was it about this hardened heart that exasperated, irritated and roused God to such a degree of indignation (*"provoke"*)? We are told that it happened *"in the day of temptation."* They began to tempt and prove God. To 'tempt God' means to desire Him to act in a way that is outside of His character. God is a holy God, but they wanted Him to accept them just the way they were. NOTE: **We do not prove the Lord!** The only thing you are ever told to prove God in is tithing (Mal.3:10). At no other time (nor issue) are we to prove God as if He is a God to be told what to do, or to be tested. If we expect God to accommodate our lifestyle, that is a hardened

heart! This is the first great danger: if you think God is going to revolve around you or accommodate the Gospel to you, then your heart is hard. This could have been cured by listening to what the Spirit of God was saying. To do so will keep your heart from hardening.

2. (3:10) *"Wherefore I was grieved with that generation, and said, They do alway err in their heart; and they have not known my ways."* The second stage of unbelief is **an erring heart,** which means a heart that keeps going astray, which is deceived or seduced time after time from the right way of the Lord. Such a heart reveals that it does not know the way of the Lord. Such a heart grieves God. **If you do not want to keep going off track, do not allow your heart to be hardened to God's voice.**

3. The third stage is **an evil heart**. *"Take heed, brethren, lest there be in any of you an evil heart of unbelief, in departing from the living God"* (3:12). Unbelief will cause an evil heart. An evil heart is a heart that departs from God into utter unbelief. This does not happen overnight. It starts with a hardened heart in tempting God. It then manifests in constant erring with no knowledge of God's true way. Then finally it takes its last form in a departure from God.

Unbelief kept them out of the Promised Land. Even though they knew that God had sworn to give them the land and that He was not a man that He should lie, they still acted in unbelief. God was calling them to trust Him, to have faith in Him and because He wanted them to trust Him. God swore to Abraham, to Isaac, to Jacob, to Joseph, and all the way down the line to give future generations a strong basis upon which to rest their faith. God was trying to bring them to a place of strong faith and confidence in knowing that He would do what He said. God is now trying to bring you and me to a place where we are not going to doubt Him. He wants to bring you to a place where you are not going to be weighed down with all sorts of strife, as you wonder, "Will He really carry me through? Will He really do what He has promised? Do I really trust that HE can get me through this wilderness? Do I really know that He is going to keep me and stop me from falling? Do I know that He will keep me from the Devil?"

God wanted to bring the whole nation of Israel to a place of strong faith, yet ten days across that wilderness on the edge of the Promised Land, they felt compelled to send 12 spies into the Land. The Lord had promised the land to them. He had told them what it was like. God had commanded them to go in, but here they are testing God instead of just believing what He had said. They were testing His word. As a result ten spies return with an evil report and two with a good report. Ten had an evil heart of unbelief. They said, "We cannot!" because they were moved by the natural element of man: their eyes; what they saw; what they heard. They looked at the giants and the great walls and said, "It is impossible! We cannot!" They were right! *They* could not because their faith was not in God. Their eyes were not on God. But two men, Joshua and Caleb, said, "We are well able to go into the land," because their eyes were not on the giants or the size of the walls; their eyes were on God. Their eyes were looking back through time to God's Word given to the Patriarchs, knowing that God swore to Abraham and to Isaac and to Jacob; knowing that they had the promises of God. God promised to give them all that land and destroy all their enemies. God said, "I want to give it unto you, so just trust me! Have faith in me!"

God was trying to bring Israel to faith yet only two men believed. God got angry with Israel. He said, "I wanted to show you a land (life) that you were going in to possess but you mixed unbelief with my Word. You did not believe my Word. You said, 'it is impossible'."

Are you saying that in your heart and mind? Are you hearing what Paul is saying to the Hebrews warning them about unbelief? Here are two to three million people who will walk in that wilderness for forty years where they will die because of unbelief. Only two of that old generation walked out of that wilderness because they said, "We are well able." Their faith was tried for 40 years. Their faith was tested by fire.

After 45 years, Caleb said, "Give me this mountain!" He had the same faith. He was utterly convinced. He had faith in his heart. Because of the faith in God that was in his heart he was still as strong, as fresh and as envisioned as all those years previously when he was young. Faith kept him and preserved him through that long wilderness journey.

Hebrews holds forth a terrible warning concerning unbelief! Paul is writing to New Testament churches in the first century and this is the warning he gives them: millions of people who had God's Word, who were given God's promises, did not mix faith with the Word so they died in the wilderness. What a warning!

God wants to settle your mind and your heart, and bring you to a place of faith.

WHAT IS FAITH?

Hebrews 3:6 *"But Christ as a son over his own house; whose house are we, if we hold fast the confidence and the rejoicing of the hope firm unto the end."* Faith is a confidence. You do not have faith if you do not have confidence in holding fast until the very end. It is not enough that you believe for a year or five years: it is holding fast until that day that you see Christ. True faith holds on and will not let go of God no matter what it sees, hears or feels. True faith remains firm to the end.

Hebrews 11:1, *"Now faith is the substance of things hoped for, the evidence of things not seen."* Faith IS something and we need to know what it is. *"...faith is the substance of things hoped for..."* Hope is always in the future; hope is looking forward to something with expectation. Hope makes you glad as you look away from present circumstances to future things. Hope is a future expectation. Hope is a desire to see the promises of God fulfilled in your life and to possess what they reveal. So when you have hope towards God, you are hoping that He will do what He has said and move in your life. You are hoping and trusting one day you will be with Him. You are hoping to be filled with the Holy Ghost. Hope is not something vague and uncertain but it is a lively sure expectation. But hope without faith is lacking. It is not enough just to hope. You may say, "I hope God will answer me", or, "I hope God will save me", or, "I hope God will use me," or, "I hope I will be filled with the Holy Ghost," or, "I hope that I will get healed." But that is not enough, that is not sufficient—faith is the substance of hope. Hope will not of itself bring something to you or make the Word of God a reality in your life. Hope is future and you will never attain unto it without faith. Hope by itself is never sufficient. Without hope, faith is empty but faith puts substance in the hand of hope. Hope can suddenly falter. You have hoped for things that did not happen and that put you in a dilemma. We are told in Proverbs 13:12, *"Hope deferred maketh the heart sick: but when the desire cometh, it is a tree of life."* To be deferred means to delay, extend, to stretch out, or to take a long time. Hope without faith will become sick through long delay.

"When a wicked man dieth, his expectation shall perish: and the hope of unjust men perisheth." (Proverbs 11:7) A wicked man hopes that when he dies 'that everything will be ok'; they hope that their sins will not catch up with them. Religious people have an expectation that God will accept them into Heaven; habitual unrepentant sinners hope that they will make it and be accepted because 'God is a God of love and forgives everyone.'

But the Bible says that their expectation will perish at the point of death. Hope without true faith in God will perish; it is empty. Hope without faith will put a man in Hell.

Many people confuse presumption for faith. Presumption is a belief without evidence. It is believing something that is not based upon the written Word of God. You presume something for no reason, or you presume without foundation. A presumptuous person does not use their mind or seek out the facts. They are in utter ignorance. They can pick up an opinion without weighing it up and drop it just as quickly. This is not the same as faith. Presumption has no foundation or substance to rest on. Presumptuous people are shallow. Their heart has not been searched to the depths. Presumption is confidence in nothing. Presumption has no real substance. Presumptuous people do not know what they believe or why they believe.

"Now faith is the substance of things hoped for." (Heb.11:1) Faith is something; it is the actual substance of hope. This word **Substance** (*hupostasis*) means, 'standing under or to be established under'; it is talking of the ground, the basis or the support that goes under something to uphold it. It is the exact

opposite of that which is unreal, imaginary or deceptive.

'Faith substantiates hope'. Faith is the ground for our confidence. Faith gives you a good, solid place to stand. It is a firm persuasion. It gives you an assurance of heart. It is the ground of expectation. It gives us a reason and solid ground upon which to hope that things that are unseen will come to pass. Faith is the assurance of things hoped for; it substantiates or gives substance to our hope. It is a firm persuasion of things hoped for. It brings a confidence, assurance, persuasion, steadfastness and rest to the heart. It convinces me and makes me certain. It puts our feet upon firm ground while waiting for the fulfilment of God's promises. Faith deals with evidence, fact and foundation. Faith is substance. Faith tells you it is an absolutely certain, settled thing. John 6:69, *"And we believe and are sure that thou art that Christ, the Son of the living God."* Every true convert who believes receives a full assurance concerning who Christ is.

Faith always has a reason for its strong conviction. He goes further in saying that, *"faith is...the evidence of things not seen."* It is the evidence of things we cannot see with our natural eye; things that we cannot feel with our hands; things that we cannot hear with our natural ears; but faith gives you evidence of those things which are not seen and proves that they are real. The word *"evidence"* (*elegchos*) means proving or proof. It means to convince through demonstration, or to be the means of proof, or that which convinces one of something. It is the proof of things which you cannot see with your natural eye. Faith will bring you to an absolute confident assurance about things that cannot be seen with the naked eye. Faith is what enables you to see afar off those things which are invisible, eternal, spiritual and unchanging. Faith is like a telescope or binoculars. Faith opens the spiritual eyes to see and to be convinced of things which are hidden to the natural eye. There is no such thing as blind faith.

This word *"evidence"* also means reproof. It means 'reproof' because every doubt, skepticism or blindness against what the Bible says will be rebuked by faith. Faith rebukes what atheism says. Faith rebukes what evolution says. Faith rebukes what man says. Real faith is raised up upon evidence and facts. It gives proof that those things which you cannot see are real. Again, faith is built on evidence. Never say that faith is merely mystical or an emotional feeling. Faith persuades me that the born-again experience is true. Faith persuades me that the worst, vilest of sinners can be saved. Faith persuades me that God created all things.

We are told that it was by faith that Moses *"...endured, as seeing him who is invisible"* (11:27). Faith opened his eyes to see God and as a result he pressed on through the trials and past the impossibilities and accomplished remarkable things for God. It was all because faith gave him absolute evidence to put his hope in and through more that forty years of real life and overwhelming tasks we see vividly just how real that faith was. It was not a mirage, it was not make believe, it was not mind over matter; it was the real substance of real faith. Faith proves that unseen things are REAL. You cannot exercise faith without evidence. God does not expect you to believe in a mirage. He does not expect you to believe in nothing. **Men who saw a mirage and only ever relied on their natural sight and feelings in a desert, perished.** Whether natural or spiritual this principle applies.

Faith is not vague. It is not a case of, "Well, we just have to hope." Faith is not supported by nothing—faith is very solid and is supported by God Himself and is more real than the things that surround you. Faith does not live by the natural five senses. It does not put its confidence in the natural, material, physical, temporary, changeable things of this world. It is solidly based upon God Himself and His written Word. *"For we walk by faith, not by sight"* (II Cor.5:7).

Hebrews 11:2, *"For by it the elders obtained a good report."* It was by faith that all the great men and woman of the Bible obtained a good report. By faith they ran well and finished well. By faith they obeyed God. By faith they accomplished things that man and natural sense would have said was impossible. By faith they obtained a good report from God in Heaven. And now they have obtained a good report in the Church of Jesus Christ, all because they put their faith in God alone.

CHAPTER 4

DOCTRINE OF BAPTISMS

Hebrews 6:1-3, *"Therefore leaving the principles of the doctrine of Christ, let us go on unto perfection; not laying again the foundation of repentance from dead works, and of faith toward God, Of the **doctrine of baptisms**, and of laying on of hands, and of resurrection of the dead, and of eternal judgment. And this will we do, if God permit."*

Just as true **repentance** leads to true **faith** so also true faith leads to true **baptisms**. These foundations build upon each other and merge into each other. Repentance from dead works will lead to faith toward God; **the doctrine of baptisms** will lead to the laying on of hands; and the doctrine of resurrection of the dead will lead to eternal judgment.

But the very first place that the newly repented believer will come to on the highway of walking with Christ is the place of baptisms. Mark 16:16 says, *"He that **believeth** and is baptized shall be saved; but he that believeth not shall be damned."* So we see that baptism comes after believing. When you believe you then get baptized. It also says *"he that believeth not shall be damned."* Note, it does not say that he who is **not** baptized will be damned, but he who does not **believe** will be damned. So baptism is not essential for salvation. It is however vital and important and is the first act of faith and discipleship. After meeting Christ, baptism is the first act of faith and discipleship you come to. Show me someone who does not get baptized and you show me someone who will not grow in Christ. If you really believe in Christ you will get baptized in water. Baptism is an outward act to show that you have really repented and believed in your heart.

Again, if you never get baptized in water you will not be damned eternally. Two thieves hung dying on two crosses either side of Christ on Golgotha. Both were reviling and scorning him but suddenly one of those thieves changed and came to believe that Christ was the Messiah and put his faith in Christ. He turned from being an utter sceptic to one who believed. Was that thief baptized? No, but he believed in Christ for just those few hours before dying yet Christ assured him that on that very same day he would be with Him in Paradise. That thief could not get baptized; he could not go and evangelise; he could not do any good works and he had nothing to merit him; but it was by faith that he was saved—not baptism. **Understand though that baptism is one of the foundations of our faith and is vital for spiritual growth, but not vital for spiritual birth.**

Peter the apostle[4], preaching to great crowds in the street as recorded in Acts 2:38 and 41, said, *"**Repent** and be baptized every one of you in the name of Jesus Christ for the remission of sins, and ye shall receive the gift of the Holy Ghost...Then they that gladly received his word were baptized."* We saw from the scripture in Mark that baptism was the first act of faith after believing, but we also see here that baptism is the first outward act after repenting. If you repent of your sins, then be baptized in water. Note, these were people who heard the Gospel, repented, and immediately responded by being baptized all on one day. Faith came into their hearts after they came under conviction of sin and really repented. They were then immediately baptized.

What does the word Baptism mean? We cannot take our definition from tradition or the contemporary Church. Infant baptism is a man-made tradition and is not Scriptural at all. Infant baptism in fact reveals a lack of understanding of what 'baptism' actually is and means.

The Greek word is *baptizo* and appears 77 times in the New Testament. As a word it carries the following meanings:

- To dip repeatedly, to **immerse**, to submerge; (in other words no part of the body is left above the water)
- To moisten; to be soaked with; (if you are not soaked you have not been baptized)

---

[4] He is Peter the apostle, not the Apostle Peter: being an apostle is not a title, it is a gifted ministry. No gifted ministry is used as a title anywhere in the Bible.

- To **cover wholly with fluid**; to cleanse by dipping; to wash;
- Overwhelm; to plunge beneath;

From this we can see that Baptism does not mean 'to sprinkle' water upon or to 'pour' water. The word for, *'sprinkle'* is *rhantizo* (Heb.9:13), and the word for *'pour,'* is *Ekcheo* (Acts 2:17; Tit.3:6). They are utterly different words and have utterly different meanings to *baptizo*.

Baptism or *baptizo* was used in the following ways in the Greek language:

i) **For the sinking of a ship**: i.e. you cannot see the vessel at all; it has disappeared from sight below the surface of the water. In other words Baptism is **TO LOSE SIGHT OF WHO YOU ARE.**

ii) **For dipping animals**: in order to kill all the infections, parasites and bugs, the animal has to be dipped which means having its whole body submerged and soaked in the dip otherwise it will die of disease.

iii) **For the washing or dyeing of clothes:** you cannot sprinkle water on a dirty garment and hope that it gets clean or sprinkle dye on a garment and hope that it changes colour evenly. There is no point saying you have washed or dyed those garments if you have only sprinkled them with water.

iv) **For soaking food:** we soak chickpeas overnight in water in order to soften them for consumption— sprinkling would not accomplish this.

v) **For being submerged in a river**: the word was frequently used in the Greek language to simply describe a person submerged in a river; this is exactly its literal meaning.

All of the above examples and illustrations of baptism prove that baptism CANNOT mean sprinkling. 'Christening' or baptising a baby is not Scriptural. It is a man-made tradition. A baby has not repented, a baby has not come to faith, and a baby cannot listen to the Word of God. God could not have been clearer in what He intends for us with regards to baptism: He intends that it is an utter soaking and saturation taking place after repentance and faith.

Why is this point of sprinkling versus immersion so important? Well, if the notion of 'sprinkling' ever took root in your mind then it will affect everything in your Christian walk. When it comes to being baptized in the Holy Ghost, you might settle for a sprinkle of the Spirit instead of being immersed in the Spirit. That makes a massive difference. The same goes for repentance: a sprinkling of repentance is very different than a biblical baptism of repentance. We will see this as we go further in this doctrine of baptisms.

THE DOCTRINE OF BAPTISMS

The Catholic Church, and even some Pentecostals, have made baptism a requisite for salvation but we shall fully prove in this message that this is contrary to what we read in the Bible. Baptism is not essential for salvation. However, we must stress that the **doctrine of baptisms** must be in place if you are going to grow—not the *act* of baptism but the doctrine of baptisms. This is confirmed all through the New Testament. The word *"doctrine"* simply means *teaching*. And please note the plural, *"baptisms"*—it means more than one baptism. So it is the **teaching of baptisms** which is foundational. In the early Church every new believer was taught about these various baptisms.

WHAT ARE THESE MANY BAPTISMS?

1. JOHN'S BAPTISM
John's doctrine or teaching was a **baptism of repentance**. John taught a doctrine of repentance; John taught an absolute baptism of repentance; a life immersed in repentance: to repent for their thoughts; their attitudes; their actions; they had to repent for every area of their lives. No area of the life escapes baptism. When you come to Christ every area of your life is going to be dealt with. God graciously reveals areas of our lives which need to be baptized in repentance. When the Spirit of God begins to deal with you over a particular sin, it will almost feel like an unforgiveable sin even though others might think nothing of it. There are things in the past that you will never do again. When you suddenly begin to grieve over things in your life, and you

begin to wonder why you ever did them, this is a baptism of repentance. A baptism of repentance will wash through all your life, your home, your workplace and will flow into every decision you make. In every area of your life, repentance will come knocking on your door saying, "I am going to break in the door. Break into your plans, your thoughts, and your decisions. I am going to change everything." That is what repentance does. It affects and changes everything.

Think about John the Baptist for a moment. No one ever went up to him on the banks of the Jordan and said, "Here, John, I'm going to tell you a joke." No one entered into a bit of light chat with John. John would burn and scorch you; he was a blazing fire. He was the embodiment of what true repentance was. Repentance scorches you, changes you, and radically turns you around.

Luke 7:30, *"But the Pharisees and lawyers rejected the counsel of God against themselves, being not baptized of him."* The Pharisees and lawyers cast aside John's message of repentance, they wanted an outward religion without inward repentance, good deeds without a pure heart, a sprinkle of religiosity without a radical inward baptism that would utterly change their hearts. In Mark 11:30, Christ puts them on the spot by asking them, *"The baptism of John, was it from heaven, or of men? answer me."* They refused to answer because they were scared of the people, but by their lives and actions it was obvious that they had rejected the baptism of repentance and neutralized its message.

2. BAPTISM OF SUFFERING
Matthew 20:20–24 *"Then came to him the mother of Zebedee's children with her sons, worshipping him, and desiring a certain thing of him. And he said unto her, What wilt thou? She saith unto him, Grant that these my two sons may sit, the one on thy right hand, and the other on the left, in thy kingdom. But Jesus answered and said, Ye know not what ye ask. Are ye able to drink of the cup that I shall drink of, and to be baptized with the baptism that I am baptized with? They say unto him, We are able. And he saith unto them, Ye shall drink indeed of my cup, and be baptized with the baptism that I am baptized with: but to*

sit on my right hand, and on my left, is not mine to give, but it shall be given to them for whom it is prepared of my Father. And when the ten heard it, they were moved with indignation against the two brethren." [Also recorded in Luke.12:50].

The Mother of Zebedee's children (James and John)asks Christ if her two boys may sit at His right and left hand in the coming kingdom. (Mothers are very influential; when they knock on Heaven's door in prayer, God is going to have trouble with that mother until He answers her. Women are born determined and mothers will not let go of a cause...). Jesus answers her with a question: 'Can your two sons be baptized with the baptism with which I am to be baptized?' That mother is quick to speak and readily replies that they can. But Christ is talking about the baptism of suffering; of going to the Cross and dying. If a man does not suffer he is not going to sit on any throne. There is going to be a baptism of death and what Christ refers to later in this chapter is His betrayal and death on the Cross where He is to be baptized in a baptism of suffering and death. Christ is going to be utterly baptized into a baptism of death. He will suffer mentally and emotionally. He is going to travail in the garden of Gethsemane. So Christ is asking James and John if they are willing to come this way of baptism. If you want to sit on a throne, you will go through that garden of Gethsemane. James did die a martyr's death and John was put in a pot of hot oil but escaped out of it and ended up on the island of Patmos as a prisoner of Rome when over 90 years of age. They did go through a baptism of suffering.

Christ may ask one of you to drink from the cup of suffering that He drank from in order that you might rule with Him. What if all the rewards and blessings mean the loss of your life? Or the laying down of your life physically? Christ does not choose that for everyone, but that is for some. We have lost that martyr spirit in this hour. No one wants to suffer for preaching the Gospel.

I know a preacher who has stood outside homosexual bars and nightclubs witnessing, and has often been punched in the face, but he simply turns the other cheek and says, "Do you want to hit the other cheek?" He never reacts to the violence shown to him or retaliates or lifts his hand but continues to preach the Gospel. Whilst we do not go looking for that, we have lost that baptism of death and that ability to suffer for Christ. We are so weak that a headache heralds the end of our world. We get some pressure put on us and suddenly everything becomes doom and gloom and our faith begins to crumble. But there is a baptism of death that will raise faith in our hearts to endure through suffering.

Again, this teaching of a baptism of death or suffering is essential or foundational to our walk with Christ. If we know from the beginning of our walk that there is a baptism of suffering, then we will not *count it a strange thing* when we suffer or when we pass through things that we do not understand. You do not need to know the reason why, but you must lay hold of Christ in it. Paul was very clear in teaching this to all the gentile churches, *"...exhorting them to continue in the faith, and that we must through much tribulation enter into the kingdom of God"* (Acts 14:22).

3. BAPTISM INTO CHRIST

Baptized into Christ – put on Christ (Gal.3:27). *"For as many of you as have been baptized into Christ have put on Christ."* What does it mean to be baptized into Christ? It means your whole life—every area—gets baptized into Christ. This is being submerged or lost in Christ. You do not have the right to live your life outside of Christ. He died for you. He paid the price of blood for you. He suffered for you on the Cross. Now He asks that you lose your life in Him. That does not mean that you lose your personality; that does not mean that you lose who you are; you do not lose your sense of responsibility but your whole life becomes merged with Him so that you will not, or you cannot make decisions outside of Christ—this is salvation. The born-again experience is a baptism into Christ. The Holy Spirit takes a man from darkness to light; He submerges that man into Christ. We lose our own identity outside of Christ. We no longer live our life outside of Christ. Everything that we do is inside Christ. We have put on Jesus; we have been baptized into Him.

Baptized into His death, burial, and resurrection **Romans 6:3–4**
"Know ye not, that so many of us as were baptized into Jesus Christ were baptized into his death? Therefore we are buried

69

with him by baptism into death: that like as Christ was raised up from the dead by the glory of the Father, even so we also should walk in newness of life. " We must die to our own ambitions, our own will. Christ had to lay aside His own will; leave the glory and splendour of Heaven where He had perfect fellowship with His heavenly Father because He wanted to save you. Christ hung on a Cross between Heaven and Earth and men made a mockery of Him. Men who had hardly lived 30 years told Him to save Himself if He was truly the Messiah. They ridiculed Him. And all of this, He suffered for you and me. For the first time in all of Eternity He experienced His Father looking away from Him as our sin was placed upon Him. He did not become a sinner, but He became an offering for our sin (Heb.10:8 & 18). He went through suffering we cannot imagine when our sin rested upon Him.

When we are baptized into His death Christ calls us to count the cost to follow Him. Death will come knocking on every area of your life. He will ask you to die to your own will, your own ambition, your pride, your job, your boyfriend, or girlfriend; die to getting your own way and all the things you covet after.

The baptism into Christ's burial means that when someone comes and kicks us, calls us a name or slanders us, we do not move because we are dead and buried. A dead man does not react. A dead man does not speak. You will be able to walk through situations which are not normal because it is Christ that is bringing you into identification with Himself that you can walk through these things. You should have un-forgiveness in your heart but you do not have it; you should have anger welling up but you don't; you should be fretting and pulling your hair out but you are at peace. Being baptized into Christ is a place of safety and security. That old flesh life is not safe: it gets angry; it complains; it gets upset; frustrated and discouraged. But just allow the experience of this baptism in Christ to work in you and through you and everything is utterly different. *Me in Him and Him in me.*

But please note that we are also baptized into His resurrection. This means that when we lay down our own life through the work of the Cross that we will be raised by the glory of our Father to walk in newness of life. In this baptism we gain more than we lose. A new life lived in resurrection power.

Baptized into the body of Christ (the Church) I Cor.12:13, *"For by one Spirit are we all baptized into one body...and have been all made to drink into one Spirit."* When you are put into Christ or baptized into Christ by the same Spirit you are baptized into the body of Jesus Christ: the Church. So to join the church you did not have an 'initiation' or have to fill in a form or sign on the dotted line; the Spirit of God took you and baptized you into the body of Christ. Before being born-again you were baptized or immersed in your own life but suddenly you become part of a family: the body of Christ. Christ has put you in a place you did not have before. You are no longer an orphan or an outsider. You are made a part of the body of Christ by a supernatural work of God. Some are a hand, some a foot, some a tongue, some an eye or an ear—we are all different members, we are made **a particular member** of the body by Christ. If you are wondering, "What is my place in this church?" just allow the Spirit of God to function in you. He will make you operate as a part of the body. You do not need to strive to attain to anything; you just need to walk with Christ. If you allow His life to flow in you, you are going to find your place in the church. No leader or preacher can make you a member of the church or make you function in a certain way in the church. Only the Spirit of God can make you what you are meant to be in the church. God has a place for each one who have truly repented and believed on Christ.

Many Evangelical churches which do not believe in the baptism of the Holy Spirit will teach that this scripture is talking about the baptism in the Holy Spirit but please note that it is not. They say that by one Spirit we are all baptized into one body which is the 'baptism in the Holy Spirit'. But this scripture has NOTHING to do with the Baptism in the Holy Ghost because it is CHRIST who baptizes you in the Holy Ghost. This however, is the Holy Spirit taking you and placing you into the body of Christ as a member and this happens at salvation. In Ephesians 4:5, we read of the *"one baptism"*. This is the *one baptism* because it is **absolutely essential for salvation.** Remember baptism in water is not essential for salvation. Neither is the baptism in the Holy Spirit essential for salvation, but this one baptism of being **baptized into the body of Christ is an absolutely essential** event that happens at the point of true salvation.

4. BAPTISM IN WATER

We all know that the Catholic Church, as well as the churches which came out of her around the time of the Reformation, 500 years ago—the Lutheran, the Anglican, the Reformed churches—all sprinkle babies with water. Even the great Methodist Church birthed out of revival in the 18th century carried on the same practice. The Eastern Orthodox Church have it half correct because they fully immerse the baby, but from what we have already studied we know this is not *baptism in water* because repentance and faith must precede true baptism. If you were baptized as a baby it counts for nothing; you must be baptized after you get saved. When you get baptized as an adult, you are not getting 're-baptized' because that which took place as a baby cannot be recognized as a baptism at all.

One of the old church fathers, Cyril of Jerusalem, wrote in 348 A.D: "As he who is *plunged in the waters* and baptized, is **encompassed** [utterly covered] by the water on all sides, so they that are baptized by the Spirit are also covered all over." So into the fourth century they still believed in full immersion. Many other quotes from the third and fourth centuries exist to show that this was still practised. But in the second century AD there are records of new believers who were so sick they were about to die, who could not get to the baptismal tank or river, so they came up with an idea (beware of man's ideas!), they said, "Let's just do this for our sick brethren. We'll bring the water in and sprinkle them and pour some on their heads." This satisfied them and they called it a baptism. This is where this church tradition started and it soon extended to the babies. The babies had to be sprinkled in order 'to be saved'. Baptism is not a sacrament as the Catholic Church like to call it; Baptism is an ordinance. There are many truly, born-again believers who still believe that children must be sprinkled but again Scripture makes it clear: *"John was baptizing in Enon, near to Salim, because there was much water there"* (Jn.3:23). John needed very much water because he needed to fully immerse men and women. They surely knew that they had been under the water.

Matthew 3:16, *"And Jesus, when he was baptized, went up straightway out of the water:"* Jesus Himself was in the water when He received baptism. He was not just sprinkled. Acts 8:38-39, *"They went down into the water, **both** Philip and the eunuch, and he baptized him. And when they were come up out of the water..."* The one being baptized and the one baptising were both down there in the water. This was a real New Testament baptism.

The Qualifications for Being Baptized in Water:
i) Receive the Word of God (Acts 2:41; 16:14-15; 19:5). Lydia's heart was opened to believe the Word which she had heard spoken. God must open the heart to believe His Word. There has got to be a hunger for the Word. If someone has not got a hunger for the Word, they are not a candidate to be baptized; they are not truly born-again.
ii) Repent (Acts 2:37-38). This is absolutely essential. If you experience baptism in water before you experience repentance then it was not a true baptism. Baptism in water follows after genuine heart repentance.
iii) Believe (Mk.16:15-16; Acts 8:12-15; 35-38). Faith always goes before baptism and the first act of faith after salvation is to obey God's Word in being baptized.
iv) A Good conscience *"The like figure whereunto even baptism doth also now save us (not the putting away of the filth of the flesh, but the answer of a good conscience toward God,) by the resurrection of Jesus Christ"* (I Pet.3:21). Peter talks about those who get baptized: it is the *answer of a good conscience*. There is a witness in their hearts which says, "I am born-again. I want to live for Jesus." They are not absolutely perfect on every issue, but they have a good conscience: their conscience has been made right and they respond in being baptized.
v) Disciple of Christ. Matthew 28:19, *"Go ye therefore, and teach all nations, baptizing them in the name of the Father, and of the Son, and of the Holy Ghost:"* True Discipleship begins in the act of obedience in being baptized in water. Nobody can say they are a true Disciple until they are baptized in water. It is the

first act of Discipleship. In the early Church, newly saved believers were baptized the same hour, the same day—they did not give those newly born-again believers time to even go home. If they were born-again on the side of a street, they would find the nearest option for baptism.

The man, through whom my Granny and Granddad were saved, was an evangelist from Waterford, Ireland, called Frank Bray. He was visiting my grandparent's house near Dromore when my Granny turned round to him and asked, "What is stopping me from being baptized today, here and now?" To which he replied, "Nothing. You've repented, you've believed, you've trusted in God—you desire nothing but Christ..." So my Granny said, "Right that's it then. We are going down the field...." and so they all walked down to the stream on our land where my granny was baptized alongside swimming geese.

5. BAPTISM IN THE HOLY GHOST

Mark 1:8, *"I* [John the Baptist] *indeed have baptized you with water: but he* [Christ] *shall baptize you with the Holy Ghost."* John is speaking of the baptism in which he baptized people physically in water but he tells of another who baptizes in the Holy Ghost. It is CHRIST who baptizes in the Holy Ghost. It is not the Holy Spirit who baptizes you in the Holy Spirit. It is Christ. Just like John took those repentant individuals and put them in water, now Jesus takes born-again believers and baptizes them in the Holy Ghost. The baptism in the Holy Ghost is Christ taking you and immersing you in the Spirit. It is not you just having an experience on a particular night with the Spirit, but it is Christ taking you and submerging you in the Holy Ghost. There is going to come a moving of the Holy Spirit on your prayer life; on your evangelism; and on your whole life. It is nothing to be worried about or scared about. He will not embarrass you although He may get you to do something which makes you lose your pride—like standing on a street corner to witness. (If you want a quick way to lose your reputation, you should stand on a street corner and preach the Gospel!)

We read in Acts 1:5, Christ speaking to the Disciples: *"For John truly baptized with water; but ye shall be baptized with the Holy Ghost not many days hence."* This is Christ speaking to men who have really failed Him. Peter denied Him, John, James and the rest fell asleep praying, yet Christ is saying to them that not many days hence they will be immersed in the Spirit. Christ is saying to Peter who denied Him to a little girl, "I am going to take you and immerse you so that you can stand up and preach the Gospel to thousands...It will not be Peter preaching out there, it will not be Peter just opening up his mouth." Remember Peter later preached to the wild mob which crucified Christ. Peter told them pointedly and publically, "YOU have crucified Christ... " Peter made it very clear to them that they were guilty of nailing Christ to the cross. Peter had to be immersed in the Holy Spirit in order to preach such an uncompromising message to that wild mob.

Acts 2:4, "*And they were all filled with the Holy Ghost, and began to speak with other tongues, as the Spirit gave them utterance.*" The baptism in the Holy Spirit is the same thing as being filled with the Holy Spirit. That which was promised in Acts 1, happened in Acts 2. The baptism in the Holy Spirit is a real experience that happens after repentance and faith.

Other Terms for being "Baptized in the Holy Spirit"
  i)   Being Filled (Acts 9:17)
  ii)   An outpouring (Acts 2:17; 10:45)
  iii) Fell upon or came upon (Acts 8:16; 11:15; 19:6)
  iv)   An enduement (a mantle or coat) of power. *Dunamis* means miraculous power (Lk.24:49; Acts 1:8).
  v)   Rivers of living water (John.7:38-39)
  vi)   The Gift of the Holy Ghost (Acts 1:45). You do nothing for a gift: it is free. You cannot earn it. You do not deserve it. Peter did not deserve it.

Baptism into the Body of Christ	By the Spirit	Into the Church/into Christ
Baptism in Water	By a preacher/believer	In Water
Baptism in the Holy Ghost	By Christ	Into Holy Ghost

If you have been baptized into the body then you should have no problem being baptized in the Spirit. You have all the faith you need; you have all the knowledge you need. These various baptisms that we have dealt with give you i) a Place in the Church, ii) Purity, in separating from the world, iii) and Power in the Holy Ghost.

EXAMPLES OF THESE DISTINCT BAPTISMS

Acts 2:4 In an Upper Room in Jerusalem, 120 people were **baptized in the Holy Ghost.** These were people who were already baptized into Christ: they were clean pure, regenerate, and born-again. They had already believed the Word, taken of the Lord's Table (Supper) and had the joy of salvation.

Acts 8 In this passage we will see three baptisms. This takes place in the City of Samaria several years after the day of Pentecost. Philip the Evangelist, a preacher, goes down to this outcast city alone. The city of Samaria was filled with half-breed people who were a mixture of Jew and Gentile and normally Jews did not go to Samaria.

    Verses 5-8, *"Then Philip went down to the city of Samaria, and preached Christ unto them. And the people <u>with one accord gave heed</u> unto those things which Philip spake, hearing and seeing the miracles which he did. For unclean spirits, crying with loud voice, came out of many that were possessed with them: and many taken with palsies, and that were lame, were healed. And there was great joy in that city."* This is salvation; this is the Gospel; this is the beginning and this is the **baptism into the body of Christ or into Christ.** The Gospel came to demon-possessed people and set them free. As you witness on the high street, as you witness to friends and family; as you are at work, this Gospel can set demon-possessed people free. If you are born-again you do have power over all the power of Hell. Just stand in Jesus' name and take authority.

    Verse 12: *"But **when they** believed Philip preaching the things concerning the kingdom of God, and the name of Jesus Christ, they were baptized, both men and women."* They had repented and believed so we see here in verse 12 they were then **baptized in water.**

Verses 14-17 *"Now when the apostles which were at Jerusalem heard that Samaria had received the word of God, they sent unto them Peter and John: Who, when they were come down, prayed for them, that they might receive the Holy Ghost: (For as yet he was fallen upon none of them: only they were baptized in the name of the Lord Jesus.) Then laid they their hands on them, and they received the Holy Ghost."* Just days or weeks after being saved and baptized in water they "received" the Holy Ghost or were baptized in the Holy Ghost.

Acts 8:26-39. Here, Philip the evangelist preaches the Gospel to the Ethiopian Eunuch who receives it readily and believes with all his heart that Jesus Christ is the Son of God. From what we have already said by believing he must have experienced a baptism of repentance, a baptism into Christ and a baptism into the body of Christ. Now he asks, *"See, here is water; what doth hinder me to be baptized?"* In preaching Christ from Isaiah 53 to this Eunuch, Philip must have mentioned or explained about baptism in water. We are then told, *"they went down both into the water, both Philip and the eunuch; and he baptized him."* This could not be clearer; both men went down into the water and standing in the water Philip baptized him. But the text is clear that he had first believed.

Acts 9:10-18. Saul (Paul) meets Christ on the road to Damascus. Saul had been saved for three days when Ananias came to see him saying, *"brother Saul"*—Saul had been baptized into Christ and the body of Christ when saved, hence Ananias calls him 'brother'. Three days earlier, Saul had been on his way to kill and destroy Ananias, but now he can call him *brother*, because Saul had repented and believed on Christ. Acts 9:17 *"...and entered into the house; and putting his hands on him said, Brother Saul, the Lord, even Jesus, that appeared unto thee in the way as thou camest, hath sent me, that thou mightest receive thy sight, and be filled with the Holy Ghost."* Again, after salvation—in this example, three days—Saul was filled with the Holy Ghost; that is baptized in the Holy Ghost. After being baptized into Christ three days earlier and after just experiencing a personal baptism in the Holy Ghost it says that he, *"arose, and* *was baptized"* which was a baptism in water.

Acts 10:44-48. Here, Peter goes to the home of the Gentile, Cornelius: *"While Peter yet spake these words, the Holy Ghost fell on all them which heard the word.* [Almost simultaneously to hearing the Gospel for the first time, they also receive the baptism in the Holy Ghost]. *And they of the circumcision which believed were astonished, as many as came with Peter, because that on the Gentiles also was poured out the gift of the Holy Ghost. For they heard them speak with tongues,* [tongues was the evidence that the Holy Ghost was poured out] *and magnify God. Then answered Peter, Can any man forbid water, that these should not be baptized, which have received the Holy Ghost as well as we?* [These believers seem to have it 'back-to-front'. They get baptized in the Holy Ghost before they were baptized in water] *And he commanded them to be baptized in the name of the Lord. Then prayed they him to tarry certain days."* Peter recognizes that they would not have received the Holy Ghost unless they were truly born-again, so he tells those with him (who were of the circumcision or the Jews) that there is nothing to stop them from being baptized in water. These gentiles got the full 'package' in one day.

We read of several cases of household salvation in the New Testament. In each case the common denominator is hearing the Word of God and believing it. Whole households turned to Christ and were then baptized in water.

- **Acts 16:14-15** Lydia and her whole household, who are all called *"brethren,"* believe and are baptized in water This is household salvation.
- **Acts 16:30-34** The Philippian Jailor and his household were all born-again and baptized in water.
- **Acts 18:8** Crispus and his house all *"believed"* and then were baptized in water.

Acts 19:1-7 The Disciples at Ephesus: *"And it came to pass, that, while Apollos was at Corinth, Paul having passed through the upper coasts came to Ephesus: and finding certain disciples,* [people who had repented and believed] *He said unto them,* [he saw something lacking in them and so he had to ask them] *Have* *ye received the Holy Ghost **since ye believed***? [There is a time period between believing and receiving the Holy Ghost] *And they said unto him, We have not so much as heard whether there be any Holy Ghost. And he said unto them, Unto what then were ye baptized? And they said, Unto John's baptism* [baptism of repentance]. *Then said Paul, John verily baptized with the baptism of repentance, saying unto the people, that they should believe on him which should come after him, that is, on Christ Jesus. When they heard this, they were baptized* [in water] *in the name of the Lord Jesus. And when Paul had laid his hands upon them, the Holy Ghost came on them; and they spake with tongues,* [baptism in Holy Ghost] *and prophesied. And all the men were about twelve."* We ought to be asking people, "Have you received the Holy Ghost since you believed? Have you received the gift of the Holy Ghost as a definite experience? Because it is for you!"

If you were baptized into anything else: into Mormonism, or as a child into Catholicism, or into another religion, you still need to be baptized in water when you put your faith in Christ.

Even in **1 John 5:8,** we see three distinct baptisms: *"And there are three that bear witness in earth, **the Spirit**, and **the water**, and **the blood**: and these three agree in one."* There is a baptism into Christ through the blood; there is a baptism in water; and there is a baptism in the Spirit. These three —Spirit, water and blood—agree as one and are a witness in the Earth.

I once knew a man who was raised in the Brethren who was a great street preacher but who fervently believed that the baptism of the Holy Ghost was only for the early Church. That is what he had been taught in church from a child. One night he was on his way home from a half night of prayer when he clearly heard a voice tell him to stop the car and get out. Three times this was repeated clearly. On the third time he was scared to delay or ignore it further so he stopped the car and got out. He was standing on the road in the middle of the night with no one around but the cows in the field beside him. He thought for a moment that he was going mad and that he was just imagining these things but suddenly the Holy Ghost fell upon him and he was baptized in the Spirit. Out of his belly flowed a river as he spoke forth in tongues. This was a radical life changing experience for this preacher. The baptism of the Holy Ghost is for every believer and will give you power to witness.

As we close, may I ask you, have you been baptized in the Holy Ghost? The gift of the Holy Ghost is for you. It is God's will that His people be submerged and drenched in the Holy Ghost.

CHAPTER 5

LAYING ON OF HANDS

As we look at foundations, let us remember that we cannot cut corners when building a house. Where too little cement was used in the building of bridges in China, the bridges collapsed. The correct proportions and ingredients must go into the foundations if the building is to stand.

Our foundations thus far have been:
1. Repentance from dead works
2. Faith toward God
3. Doctrine of baptisms
And now we come to the fourth doctrine:
4. Laying on of hands

Heb.6:1-3, *"Therefore leaving the principles of the doctrine of Christ, let us go on unto perfection; not laying again the foundation of repentance from dead works, and of faith toward God, Of the doctrine of baptisms, and of **laying on of hands**, and of resurrection of the dead, and of eternal judgment. And this will we do, if God permit."*

"Therefore leaving the principles..." Remember, this word *'principles'* means the beginnings, or ABCs. These ABCs, or foundations, must be in place if we are to go on to perfection and be mature. We cannot learn to read until we know our ABCs and in the same way we cannot grow in Christ unless we know our ABCs.

"And this will we do..." We do not want to remain static, stay where we are, or walk in circles—we want to move on. The unhappiest people in the Church are those that just get in the door and stay there. They do not go deeper in Christ and they live half in Christ and half in the world. These are the most miserable people you will ever meet because they cannot enjoy

the world—they have tasted too much of Christ to be satisfied with the world—and yet they cannot enjoy Christ because they are holding onto the world and trying to enjoy it. To go on to fullness in Christ, to a fullness of joy, to full peace and the reality of walking with Christ, they will have to let go of the world.

You cannot have one eye on the church and one eye on the world. This is what is meant by a *'double minded man'* in God's Word. This double minded man is, *"...unstable in all his ways"* because his mind is going in two different directions at the same time (Jm.1:8). This man cannot set his focus on the journey. He is trying to go to two different cities at the same time but this will result in going nowhere. The Bible says, *"...let not that man think that he shall receive any thing of the Lord"* (Jm.1:7). In his prayers that man is saying he wants the Lord, but by his lifestyle he reveals that he also wants the world. To have a divided heart is miserable and produces a lukewarm person who Christ will spew out of His mouth (Rev.3:16). Christ would rather you are boiling hot or freezing cold; either in Christ or in the world. If you play games between the two places, you will end up lukewarm, mediocre, and always vacillating.

This is NOT talking about the ups and downs or troubles of the Christian life which we all go through. No, this is a man who has not nailed his colours to the mast and said, "Christ alone for me!" This is not talking about the realm of feelings where tonight you feel on top of the mountain but tomorrow morning you wake up and all your feelings are gone so you feel that the whole world is against you and you wonder where God is. That is simply just your feelings and has nothing to do with your walk with God. Those are natural feelings. Maybe you feel blessed tonight but devastated in the morning. What happened during the night? Nothing! God did not change. Maybe in this realm of emotions, the Lord is testing you to see what your heart desires, but God has not changed.

'Laying on of Hands' is a part of the 'Doctrine of Christ' (Heb.6:1). This is a foundational doctrine for those who have been brought into Christ, brought into the Church, and brought into a life in the Spirit. This teaching is to carry you forward into maturity in Christ.

Who would have thought that the doctrine of laying on of hands was a basic teaching and a necessary foundational doctrine? I would not have, but God, by the Holy Spirit has placed it here as one of the six foundational doctrines that every Christian needs to learn from the beginning. In other words, there is something that happens in the laying on of hands. There is a ministry in the laying on of hands that is going to help you to walk with Christ. There is a spiritual effect, a power and impact when hands are laid on you in a meeting which helps you in your walk to go on into maturity in Jesus Christ. Because this doctrine appears here in Hebrews 6, God is marking it out as a vital part of your walk with Christ.

"Faith cometh by hearing and hearing by the word of God..." As we receive this teaching of the Laying on of Hands, faith will come to our hearts. As we hear about the will of God concerning the laying on of hands and as we learn the mind of God concerning it we shall come to an understanding of His purpose for it and through it, and faith will arise.

We do not *lay hands on* as some sort of ritual or because someone said we should, **we do it in response to God's Word**; God's command. Because of God's Word, I have faith that when hands are laid on me, something is going to happen. It is not empty hands on empty heads! No, when faith is involved it is hands ordained by God, laid on a head that contains a mind which fully understands what God's Word says about it.

EXAMPLES IN GOD'S WORD

Example 1: Jacob Lays Hands on his Grandsons.
Jacob was in his last days and near to death when he called Joseph to bring his two sons. Jacob [Israel] wanted to bless his two grandsons as he would his own sons. **Genesis 48:9**, *"Bring them, I pray thee, unto me, and I will bless them..."* **v14,** *"And Israel stretched out his right hand, and laid it upon Ephraim's head, who was the younger, and his left hand upon Manasseh's head, guiding his hands wittingly; for Manasseh was the firstborn."*

We see that Jacob crossed over his hands so that his right hand (the hand of greater blessing) rested on Ephraim's head (the younger of the two boys) so Joseph tried to correct the old man, but the old man had done this on purpose (*'guiding his hands wittingly'*). He knew he was laying the greater blessing upon the younger lad. Jacob blessed the boys in the name of the Lord by laying on of hands, praying, and prophesying over them. This also shows us that God had a plan for their individual lives as He does for each one of us. As Jacob laid his hands on their heads, God's plan for the boys' lives was revealed by prophecy.

"*By faith Jacob, when he was a dying, blessed both the sons of Joseph;*" (Heb.11:21) 'By faith' means this was a spiritual event; not natural, not an outward show, but Jacob was moved by faith and moved by the Holy Spirit to lay hands on these boys, to prophesy and to bring a blessing on them. It is essential to lay hands on BY FAITH. We should look for the Spirit of God to move. We should expect that God will do something real in real life situations. We need to be of faith when we lay on hands.

This custom of *laying on of hands* is still in practice amongst Jewish people today. Morning by morning the old Rabbis lay hands on the oldest to the youngest and recite the blessings of God. "God is going to bless you in your going out. God is going to bless you in your coming in. God is going to bless the labour of your hands…" They desire that God's blessing rest on each one. Wouldn't it be good if we Christians practised this?

Example 2: Moses Lays Hands on Joshua
Numbers 27:18, "*And the LORD said unto Moses, Take thee Joshua the son of Nun, a man in whom is the spirit, and lay thine hand upon him;*" v19, "*And set him before Eleazar the priest, and before all the congregation; and give him a charge in their sight.*" v20, "*And thou shalt put some of thine **honour** upon him, that all the congregation of the children of Israel may be obedient.*"

Deuteronomy 34:9, "*And Joshua the son of Nun was full of the spirit of **wisdom**; for Moses had laid his hands upon him: and the children of Israel hearkened unto him, and did as the LORD commanded Moses.*"

Moses had led around 2-3 million people for forty long

years in the Wilderness but when he was about to depart (die) he set Joshua apart for leadership by the laying on of hands. It is good to note that Joshua really was 'the son of Nun' and the son of *'none'*—in other words he thought nothing of himself but thought everything of God. Joshua was not wilful or looking for his own gain; he was a man who claimed nothing; he was simply a servant to Moses who claimed no position, power, or authority but looked for the glory of God and served Moses on a practical level in all things. But as Joshua served, he was learning from Moses. The Word tells us that when Moses left the tabernacle, Joshua was still in there seeking the Lord (Ex.33:11). Joshua had good qualifications for leadership. God acknowledged that Joshua had the Spirit dwelling in him: *"a man in whom is the spirit"* (Num.27:18). As a result of the work of the Spirit he was a spiritual man fit for the work of God. This is an essential qualification for leadership and there should be evidence of the Spirit or the Hand of God moving upon the life of a future leader.

Because Joshua is going to be the next leader in the nation, God commands that Moses is to lay his hands upon him publically: *"And set him before Eleazar the priest, and before all the congregation; and give him a charge in their sight"* (27:19). It is important for the people of Israel to see that Moses is recognizing and setting Joshua apart as a leader, so it is NOT done privately behind the scenes; It is done publically before all. Everyone then clearly understands that Joshua is a leader chosen and set in place by God through Moses.

In summary:
- God gave Joshua **honour** through the laying on of hands
- Joshua was full of the spirit of **wisdom** because he had had hands laid on him
- Moses **charged** Joshua to lead the people. The reason for this was, *"that all the congregation of the children of Israel may be obedient"* (27:20).[5]

---

[5] We should take care how we treat leaders; we should not treat them just 'any old way' and in the same way a leader should not treat the sheep just any old way. Leaders and believers must seek to abide in the

Example 3: Healing the Sick

The laying on of hands in connection with healing is not a ritual but is handed straight down to us from Christ and appears throughout Scripture.

Jairus' daughter: **Mark 5:23-42** *"And besought him greatly, saying, My little daughter lieth at the point of death: I pray thee, come and lay thy hands on her, that she may be healed; and she shall live."*(v.23) *"And he took the damsel by the hand, and said...Damsel, I say unto thee, arise. And straightway the damsel arose, and walked;"* (v.41)

Jairus' daughter was about to die; there was no hope, but Jairus knew the reputation of Jesus, that when He laid hands on the sick, they recovered. Jairus was desperate just to get Jesus to lay hands on his daughter. We are told he asks Christ, to 'lay hands' on his daughter—he does not even say, 'pray'. There was and still is just something about the touch of Christ. Christ touching you will change you spiritually, physically and emotionally—just one touch of the Master's hand will change you; revolutionize you. You cannot see His nail-pierced hands with your natural eye, but you can feel His touch, and you will never be the same. What a faith this man Jairus had.

Christ never heals without faith. No faith, no healing. Healing is not something that just floats down from Heaven. There is only one incident in the whole New Testament when faith is not mentioned in connection with healing. Faith is almost always mentioned in connection with healing.

In the healing of the Leper we read that the Leper came to Christ and asked Him, *"If thou wilt, thou canst make me clean.."* to which Christ responded, *"I will; be thou clean."* But notice what else happens: *"moved with compassion, put forth his hand, and touched him"* (Mk.1:40-41). Christ touched his leprous skin and healed him. Christ was not scared to touch the leper! He did not say go home and I will pray for you. No, He touched the Leper; He laid hands on him.

Scriptures. According to Scripture, there is a list of attitudes and manners that you ought to have toward a leader. The two extremes of abuse by leadership and on the other hand abuse of leaders by the people are both unacceptable. Responsibilities work both ways.

If you have any doubt whether God desires to heal you, then know that this is the Word of Christ Himself: "I WILL" It is Christ's will to heal every sickness. I do not understand all situations or struggles on this subject but I know it is never His will that you suffer in body, never. God is a good God and Christ is a good Christ.

Jairus knew if he could but get Christ to lay hands on his daughter that she would live. Verse 41 says, *"And he took the damsel by the hand, and said...Damsel, I say unto thee, arise. And straightway the damsel arose, and walked;"* That father's prayer was answered. God has not changed. His character or manner of operating has not changed. We do not believe in a mystical Christ who lives 'somewhere up there'. The same Christ that walked those streets over 2,000 years ago, still dwells with us and He has not changed.

The Woman Sick for 18 Years: Luke 13:11-13, *"And, behold, there was a woman which had a spirit of infirmity eighteen years, and was bowed together, and could in no wise lift up herself...said unto her, Woman, thou art loosed from thine infirmity. And he laid his hands on her: and immediately she was made straight, and glorified God."*

This woman had been sick for 18 long years. Most of us could not imagine such suffering. In a period of 18 years she had spent all her money, yet nothing had worked. For 18 long years she had suffered with a spirit of infirmity and had suffered terrible pain. We would have given up hope after 18 years of suffering. Can you imagine coming to a place of utter hopelessness after all these years of trying everything? But *"...he laid his hands on her: and immediately she was made straight, and glorified God."* God has not changed. Christ still thinks the same, acts the same and heals just the same. His power and His Will is still the same.

Is your salvation, your forgiveness, and mercy the same as it was in the Bible? YES! God still saves with the same forgiveness and mercy as He did in the Bible, and God still heals just as He did in the Bible. We experience the very same blood redemption as those people in Bible days and you can be assured that we can experience healing just as they did. *"Jesus Christ the same yesterday, and to day, and for ever"* (Heb.13:8).

In **Mark 16** we see Christ after He was raised from the dead. He is about to leave His little, weak Church and go to Heaven so He will no longer be physically or visibly with them, but the question is will He continue to do the same things once He goes to be with His Father in Heaven? Remember He told them, 'when I go I will be with you. When you go out to preach the Gospel I will be with you. I will confirm the preaching of the Gospel with signs following.' Christ says, 'When it is preached that I am there to save, I will be there to do it!' Christ is with you when you go out on to that high street to proclaim God's forgiveness. Christ is right there saying, "Amen. Amen!" He is there to respond to those who call upon Him. We do not go out on the streets by ourselves. Father, Son, and Holy Ghost stand with us as we proclaim the Gospel. The living Christ is in our midst confirming that He is the same Christ as 2,000 years ago and that He still delivers, saves and heals! Mark.16:15-18, *"Go ye into all the world, and preach the gospel to **every creature**...And these signs shall follow them **that believe**."* It does not say that these signs will follow because they call themselves, 'Christians'; it does not say that these signs will follow just because they go out. It says, *"these signs shall follow them **that believe**."* There has to be faith in the heart. There has to be a confidence and reliance upon God that He will heal.

Notice these **five supernatural signs** that follow them that believe and notice that it is not just a case of preaching the Gospel that brings such but it's to *"them **that believe**."* Christ is saying this to *all* the Church, not just to His Apostles; He says it to ALL THEM THAT BELIEVE; not to just preachers.

Now, we do not look for, or go after the signs, but if we preach the pure, simple Gospel of repentance, the Cross, the Love, Mercy and Forgiveness of God, then we ought to pray and have faith that the signs and miracles will follow. God says HE will be there to do wonders. Not you; you cannot do a thing; you and I are helpless but HE will be there to do wonders. The living Christ will be with you on those streets and these are the five supernatural signs He promises:

i)   in my name shall they cast out devils;

ii)   they shall speak with new tongues;

iii)   they shall take up serpents;

iv)   and <u>if</u> they drink any deadly thing, it shall not hurt them;[6]

v)   **they shall lay hands on the sick** and they shall recover.

This fifth sign is related to the laying on of hands. Those who believe; those who have faith, those who believe what God's Word says about this will lay their hands on the sick and they will recover. This is not a ritual. It is an act of faith. Those moved by faith in obedience to the Word will lay their hands upon the sick. Without faith it would be an empty ritual but when done in faith it is confirmed by God healing the sick.

Please note that point five **applies primarily to sinners:** you can lay hands on the sick sinner (someone not saved) and you can expect that God will move on that person. In Acts chapter 28, we read that Paul was shipwrecked and was then given lodgings on the island of Mileta, where the chief of the island was an unsaved man called Publius. It was Publius' father who lay sick and on whom Paul laid hands: *"...the father of Publius lay sick of a fever and of a bloody flux: to whom Paul entered in, and prayed, and <u>laid his hands on him</u>, and healed him."*

Now again, we are not careless or foolish about these things: you do not just go up to anybody and everybody and tell them that they are going to be healed once you lay hands on them. **We need to be led of the Spirit of God** in this. The Bible notes a number of such incidents (Acts 3:6-8, 16; 9:17-18; 14:9-10; 22:13).

---

[6] Please note the word *"if"* here. We do not throw our brain out or lose our logic when we become a Christian. We do not go and drink something deadly to prove God's Word. If someone was trying to kill an apostle, the apostle got in a basket and escaped down the other side of the wall. They were not shouting out to their pursuers, "Here I am! Come and catch me!" No, they ran in order to preserve their life. There is no foolishness in the Gospel. However, I know people who have been out preaching the Gospel on foreign fields, who have eaten or drank something deadly (they found out subsequently that someone was trying to kill them), yet it had no effect on them because God was there to confirm the Gospel preached.

I have prayed for many a sinner and God has touched and healed them. On the Army camp on which I lived for three and a half years, drunkards and womanizers would come to me for prayer. More specifically they would ask me to lay hands on them and pray for them—they were convinced that they would be healed! Often they would tell me that they believed that God was going to heal them through me. Now that's the faith of a sinner who does not know Christ as Lord and Saviour and who are rebels against God's Word. It is remarkable that God would heal a sinner not walking in obedience to Him, yet it is Biblical and factual. I saw more instantaneous healings there with those sinners than I have amongst most gatherings of believers. I wish there were more Christians who believed as strongly as those godless, drunken soldiers! They had faith that Christ still heals. I believe that this was an act of God's goodness and mercy in seeking to lead them to repentance (Rom.2:4).

Of course laying hands on the sick is also for believers and regarding this the Word of God is clear: to take full benefit from such provision one must be established in a local church. *"Is any sick among you? let him call for the elders of the church; and let them pray over him, anointing him with oil in the name of the Lord"* (Jm.5:14). The Word is clear: if you are afflicted, pray; if you are merry, sing, (Jm.5:13) but if you are sick, call for the elders. When you obey the Scriptures there is faith in your heart which moves you to ask for the Elders to lay hands on you and anoint you. You are coming unto the Lord, not unto the Elders. It is an act of faith in God and His written Word.

In closing this section, I want to reiterate that this is a basic, foundational doctrine that every new believer should be taught: to expect God to heal through the laying on of hands. They ought to be convinced that Scripture teaches that. Now let us move on to the laying on of hands for another reason.

Example 4: The Baptism of the Spirit or Being Filled with the Spirit

In Acts 8 we read of Philip who went down to Samaria where a great revival broke out. Many people believed; many were baptized in water and there was great joy and great miracles. In other words, there was a real church there! Now look at what happens, *"Now when the apostles which were at Jerusalem heard that Samaria had received the word of God, they sent unto them Peter and John: Who, when they were come down, prayed for them, that they might receive the Holy Ghost: (For as yet he was fallen upon none of them: only they were baptized in the name of the Lord Jesus.) Then laid they their hands on them, and they received the Holy Ghost"* (Acts 8:14-17). Note these believers were saved and baptized in water but they had not been baptized in the Holy Ghost, so the two Apostles laid hands on them and they received the Holy Ghost. The Apostles went to Samaria with faith in their hearts that they were going to see that church in Samaria come into the baptism of the Holy Ghost. They knew that those new believers were filled with joy over their salvation, but they wanted to see them baptized in the Holy Ghost and this they did by the laying on of hands. Remember, great miracles had already been done in their midst; Christ had changed their whole community, yet those two Apostles knew that they needed to go and lay hands on them to receive the Holy Ghost. Many people would be happy to halt where the church of Samaria was before they were baptized in the Holy Ghost. They would happily say, 'My life is changed. I have great joy. I know I am saved. I have seen great miracles. What more is there?' There is more. There is the baptism in the Holy Ghost!

Another example is that of Saul of Tarsus. On his way to Damascus he had an encounter with Jesus Christ and was born-again. He was then taken to Damascus where he remained blind for three days. During these days he must have sat in stunned awe as he came to terms with what had happened and his new vision of his past condition. He must have considered how many Christians he had killed. He must have been devastated and shocked! His whole life was ripped apart (Salvation can rip your whole world apart and turn it upside down you know!). Until three days before he had been coming to that community to kill Christians but then he found out that Christ was real and as a result he must have been in shock. There were no believers with him and he knew none to call on. Saul sat in that physical state of darkness praying unto God.

So Christ went to a disciple—not a preacher or an Apostle—a disciple, a Christian, named Ananias, and Christ woke him in the middle of the night to give him specific instructions (God can give any genuine believer such accurate instructions). He then sent Ananias to the very street and house where Saul was and told him to lay hands upon him. Note, that God gave Saul (Paul) the exact vision too with the detail of the name of the man who would lay hands on him. *"...And hath seen in a vision a man named Ananias coming in, and <u>putting his hand on him, that he might receive his sight</u>"* (Acts 9:12).

In verse 17 we see Ananias obeying God's instruction, *"...And Ananias went his way, and entered into the house; and <u>putting his hands on him</u> said, Brother Saul, the Lord, even Jesus, that appeared unto thee in the way as thou camest, hath sent me, <u>that thou mightest receive thy sight, and be filled with the Holy Ghost</u>"*, v18, *"...And immediately there fell from his eyes as it had been scales: and he received sight forthwith, and arose, and was baptized."* God works in such ways: if He says it, it will be *exactly* as He says! God is not a liar. We are not playing mystical games. Both men were shown exactly the same dream. In this one meeting between these two men, Saul is shown what the true Church is:

i) Ananias calls him, *"brother Saul"*, showing Saul that he is now in a family
ii) Ananias lays hands on Saul to be healed and he was healed
iii) Ananias lays hands on Saul to be baptized in the Holy Ghost and he was filled with the Spirit
iv) Saul is then baptized in water

Thank God that the very first Christian that Saul (Paul) ever met was a man obedient to Jesus Christ.

A third example from the book of Acts in which we see believers receiving the Holy Ghost through the laying on of hands is in chapter 19, when Paul goes to Ephesus. *"And when Paul had <u>laid his hands upon them</u>, the Holy Ghost came on them; and they spake with tongues, and prophesied"* (Acts 19:6). These 12 disciples in Ephesus were baptized in water by Paul. He then laid hands upon them and the Holy Ghost came upon them. **We are to expect the baptism of the Holy Ghost through the laying on of hands.**

Example 5: The Ordination of Deacons

In Acts 6, we read of the time when thousands had come to Christ and the Apostles were very busy teaching the Word of God daily. But at this time an administrative problem arose amongst the Greek widows. God gave wisdom to the Apostles in seeking to find men who would be given to the task of feeding the widows so that they could be free to give themselves continually to prayer and the study and ministry of God's Word. Prayer and the Word of God were the most vital things in that church in Jerusalem so God moved them to appoint others to take care of the sensitive time-consuming issue with the widows. Verse 3, *"Wherefore, brethren, look ye out among you seven men of honest report, full of the Holy Ghost and wisdom, whom we may appoint over this business."* If the preacher or teacher has to leave the Word of God or prayer to sort out practical problems there will be serious consequences. So we see in Acts 6:6, that deacons were appointed or ordained by the laying on of hands: *"Whom they set before the apostles: and when they had prayed, they laid their hands on them."*

Now two of these men were Philip and Stephen who were later given gifted ministries and who were used in performing great miracles, but they first served in handing out bread. Note that to do this practical job they had to be filled with the Holy Ghost and they had to be upright men. If you are a gossip I would not want you to vacuum the floor. If you are a twister, a backbiter, a liar, or a cheat, I would not want you to clean the toilets. You are not fit for it. You are not spiritual enough. If you are causing disputes and divisions, take your name off the cleaning roster (Rota). **Such principles will keep the church clean!**

Note also that these 6 men were appointed and had hands laid on them PUBLICALLY. All the people were to know that the Apostles thought highly of those six men.

Example 6: The Ordination of Elders

We see this in Titus 1:5, *"...set in order the things that are wanting, and ordain elders in every city, as I had appointed thee."* The word ORDAIN which is used here is the Greek word *kathistemi*. It means to establish or set in place. Titus was to set in place elders to lead the church in each city. Then in Acts 14:23, *"And when they had ordained them elders in every church, and had prayed with fasting, they commended them to the Lord."* This word ORDAINED used here is the Greek word *cheirotoneo,* which means to stretch out or stretch forth the hand. Note, **this does not mean voting!** You will not find voting anywhere in the Bible. This *stretching forth of the hand* is not the hand going UP to vote but it is the hand going OUT to ordain. Leaders are not voted in and out. They are to be ordained of God. Neither do they choose such a position for themselves. It is men like Paul and Titus who ordain elders through the laying on of hands.

This ordination of elders comprised of setting these men in place during a time of prayer and fasting when hands were to be laid upon them. By this act they were committed into the hands of the Lord *"on whom they believed."* They need not fear. The very same one on whom they had believed, would now help them in spiritual ministry. This public laying on of the hands revealed to all that these men were set apart for leadership in the midst of the church and it was also an act of faith by all entrusting these men into the hands of the Lord who would surely help them even as He had saved them.

Example 7: Imparting of Spiritual Gifts

In Romans 1:11-12, we read that Paul went to impart *"some spiritual gift"* to the believers at Rome. In I Corinthians 1:4-9, we see that the Corinthians came *"behind in no gift."* The gifts of which he speaks are no doubt the nine gifts mentioned in chapter 12. But we read more specifically in Paul's first letter to Timothy concerning such. Paul writes to the young preacher Timothy regarding the spiritual gift that was given to him for the ministry of preaching, **by prophecy and the laying on of hands**: *"Neglect not the gift* [charisma] *that is in thee, which was given thee by prophecy, with the laying on of the hands of the presbytery"* (I Tim.4:14).

The term **presbytery** which is used here is the same as **elders** used elsewhere in the New Testament and is a synonymous term with 'Overseers' and 'Bishops'. Note: 'Bishop' is not a man with a funny hat! The word 'bishop' is the same as the word 'overseer.' The word 'presbyter' or 'elder' means *mature*. It is speaking of those who are the more mature or the most senior. This term defines that eldership are the mature leaders within an assembly. As we have previously seen such mature elders were men set apart for spiritual ministry. Paul is referring here to the leadership in the church at Lystra. He reveals that at a certain place at a specific time they had gathered around Timothy to pray for him and one of those mature men who had the gift of prophecy began to prophesy and say something like, "Timothy, you are called to ministry…" This happened elsewhere in the Bible and still happens today. God will speak through prophecy and will give a gift or reveal His will for ministry in a life by such means. Now note what happened here: it was through the medium of prophecy and the laying on of hands that a ministry gift was imparted and received. You cannot step out into spiritual ministry without a gift and a call from God. The gift enables a man by God's grace to accomplish the will of God.

Again, Paul some years later reminds Timothy, *"Wherefore I put thee in remembrance that thou stir up the gift of God, which is in thee by the putting on of my hands"* (II Tim.1:6). Paul reminds Timothy that it was not only the presbyters that had laid hands on him at that time, but Paul also laid hands on him at that same time. So we get a full picture here: Paul and the presbyters setting Timothy apart for spiritual ministry by the laying on of hands. As they do this the Spirit speaks through one of them revealing the gifted ministry he will function in and at this same moment the Lord imparts the gift (charisma) to him. The laying on of hands is important in this. It's not a dead ritual; something actually does happen.

Paul's specific purpose in mentioning this here is to remind Timothy concerning the occasion of the imparted gift, to assure him that it is still in him although dulled, and to challenge him to now actively stir it up. This 'stirring up' means to let it burn again or to bring it to full flame or to rekindle it. He is reminding Timothy of that call which came by the laying on of hands. This can happen to us: we can receive something from God but allow it to settle down or dull down to an ember. Saints in the congregation need to remain alert to the preaching of God's

Word. If you sense that the fire in the preacher is dulling down, you need to pray through for the gift within the preacher to be stirred and for the fire to return to him and burn in him more brightly. Do not let the preacher stand alone or fight alone. Stand with him in prayer.

Paul reminds Timothy that the gift has a purpose, *"This charge I commit unto thee, son Timothy, according to the prophecies which went before on thee, that thou by them mightest war a good warfare"* (I Tim.1:18). Paul reminds Timothy that Hell is against the Church and his ministry but to *'war a good warfare.'* Ministry is a battlefield. These precious prophecies were given unto him to encourage him in the ministry. Paul now reminds him of them and urges him on in fighting according to the mind of God revealed in them.

Now the context of the next Scripture is important. Paul is talking to Timothy about raising up leaders in the local churches. Both Timothy and Titus were taught and commanded to raise up local, native leaders, or 'elders,' and they were told very specifically what an elder was to be in character. (Timothy was not an elder himself, he was an apostle, and this is one of the tasks of a gifted apostle). *"Lay hands suddenly on no man, neither be partaker of other men's sins: keep thyself pure"* (I Tim.5:22). In other words, if you see a man going out and getting drunk, do not appoint him to be an Elder or Deacon. Know who the men are whom you appoint. Know their character; their lifestyle; their habits. If someone is vacillating: one minute they are saved and the next minute they are not, do not give them positions or jobs or responsibilities in the church just to keep them in the church. If you do, you are asking for trouble. These are safeguards to be observed.

A talented, young guitarist who is just saved does not go straight into the worship team. Christ saves him and brings him into the church to learn how to walk with Christ. He is not there to play his guitar for God or to display his gift to the people. No matter what your testimony—what you have been saved from—or what you can expound from the Scriptures, you have to prove that you can live this life! **It is not about what you know, or what you have been saved from, it is a question of 'do you live this life?'** Leaders, be very careful on whom you lay hands, or to whom you give a task, or who you send out in ministry!

If you were to lay hands upon someone in order to appoint them to a task in ministry while there was a known area of sin or some immature weakness in their life you make yourself a **partaker** of their sins. This word means to be in fellowship or to share in their sins. If you turn a blind eye to the condition of their life and to a particular sin you will actually become as guilty as them by ignoring it. The only way to keep yourself pure is to take great care over who you lay hands on in appointing to a task in the church.

In summary on this point:

- Do not be quick in laying hands on anyone
- You can become a partaker of someone else's sin if you do act wrongly and in haste
- If you are slow, careful and observant it will keep you pure

Example 8: Sending Forth Apostolic Workers
In Acts 13 we find five local leaders over one church and they were gifted as *"prophets and teachers"*. I know it is traditional to have one leader over a church but you will not find that anywhere in the New Testament. Here are five leaders and they are gifted differently yet work in unity in the same church. They were even of different cultural backgrounds, yet they operated in unity.

We see the church in a time of fasting and prayer—not for a need or for any specific personal purpose but to minister unto the Lord. During this time, through the gift of prophecy, the Lord spoke unto them commanding them to separate, or 'hedge off', Paul and Barnabas: *"As they ministered to the Lord, and fasted, the Holy Ghost said, Separate me Barnabas and Saul for the work whereunto I have called them"* (Acts 13:2).

Note: *"I have called them"*, means that God had already revealed this to both of them so when that prophecy came, it would not have been a surprise to either one of them. The public prophecy was a mere outward confirmation of what God had already told them personally and privately. This is the nature of true prophecy. Do not allow anyone to direct your life through prophecy: it is not true prophecy if they are trying to direct your life or manipulate you or pressurize you.

There was a short period in my life, when I was a young man, that I would walk into different meetings, in different countries and I would go and sit on the back row and the speaker, who would not have known me from Adam, would stop in the middle of preaching and prophesy the very same prophecy which I had previously received from others. It came again and again, and confirmed what God had already told me. But these public prophecies only confirmed what He had told me personally, privately and previously in my youth.

Acts 13:3, *"...And when they had fasted* [Note: this is fasting for a second time] *and prayed, and laid their hands on them, they sent them away."* So these are two men who in the local church had been gifted as a prophet and a teacher but who were now ordained as apostles. They were gifted by God but set apart to this new ministry and calling through the laying on of hands and the operation of prophecy. They were now to be sent forth or *released* to plant churches and train up leaders. **The Holy Spirit sent them but the church released them**. The church acknowledged and supported God's call.

Incidentally this is just one mark revealing how you will know a true apostle: a true apostle will leave behind him a rake of churches and leaders wherever he ministers. Also note that in the Bible the missionaries that went out were the **most mature**, the **most able** and the **most gifted**, not the youngest, most fanatical, wildest or most enthusiastic.

In conclusion, we must note that this doctrine of LAYING ON OF HANDS is a foundational truth. It is not a ritual but when during an altar time, or as led by the Spirit, or by request, a minister lays hands on someone it is for the:

i)   Healing of the sick
ii)   Baptism of the Holy Ghost
iii)   Appointment of Deacons, Elders and Apostles,
iv)   Imparting of ministry gifts and genuine spiritual gifts

CHAPTER 6

RESURRECTION OF THE DEAD

There is a world of difference between the death of the righteous and the death of the wicked. When a man who knows Christ, dies, that is not like the death of those who are lost. The world will hold a wake[7] for the dead loved-one and it will be an occasion filled with drunkenness, laughing and joking as they hope that all is well. They do not stop to think of the reality of these things. This is how the lost send their loved ones to an eternal Hell. On the contrary though, at a believer's funeral, we can look death, sorrow, grief or mourning straight in the face. Even though our heart may be wrenched and we are grieving for our loved-one, we know that one day we will see them again. We experience the full impact of grief and do not fear grief, or have to put on a 'front'. Christ wept when Lazarus died. Christ wept because He had real emotions.

We should not try to comfort believers out of their grief but we should comfort believers **in** their grief. It is not right to say, "Time to move on. You should no longer be thinking of that loved-one." We just do not see that in the Bible. Christ knew that He was going to raise Lazarus yet He wept. Christ was touched with the feeling and emotion of that loss. We also feel such. We will miss ones that die and there is nothing wrong with that.

At brother Clendennen's funeral[8], countless grown, rough, hardy men wept. They all knew that they would see him again and they all knew that he had had 87, full years, serving God for 60 of those. He was ready to go. Even so, there was a natural

---

[7] A wake is held at the time of death of a loved one. The house is open and family and friends gather into the home during the days leading up to the funeral.

[8] B.H. Clendennen (1922-2007) was founder of School of Christ International. He was a true missionary statesmen and close friend of the author.

grief and mourning that comes with death. Death is still an enemy. Death separates friend from friend, brother from brother, wife from husband. Death is not our friend. It is the last enemy that will be put down. In the meantime, death is a different experience for us as believers than for the lost, because we know that the resurrection is real; that on the third day Christ rose from the dead.

There is a resurrection awaiting us when our physical body will be resurrected, made new, and we shall dwell with God for all Eternity. What a hope we have! What a salvation God has given us! He has given us a victory over the grave, over death and over Hell. This victory is found in Christ. What a fear would be upon us this day if we knew we had to face the grave without Christ. What a fear would be upon us if we knew we had to face eternity without Christ and without each other.

Praise God that this is not a fable or myth, but it is a reality which God has brought us into by His mercy. Christ is the Way, the Truth, and the Life: Christ is the resurrection.

Hebrews 6:1-3, *"Therefore leaving the principles of the doctrine of Christ, let us go on unto perfection; not laying again the foundation of repentance from dead works, and of faith toward God, Of the doctrine of baptisms, and of laying on of hands, and of **resurrection of the dead**, and of eternal judgment. And this will we do, if God permit."*

The previous four foundations we have studied have this in common: they relate to time; they relate to the state in which we now live. We can experience or practice these principles here on Earth and during our Christian life. The next two foundations though are different in that they are experiences we are yet to have as we only experience them after the point of death.

These are two 'End-Days' (End-times or Last Days) teachings which we all must know. Many will sit and debate 'End-Days' and a thousand questions that that topic can raise, for example, 'Who is the Antichrist', or, 'What is the correct interpretation of the book of Revelation', and 'What or who is the Beast?'; 'Who or what are the Seven Heads', or, 'Where and when things are going to happen in the future', but these are not fundamental teachings on 'End-Days'. People will 'wreck their heads' trying to understand the symbolism of Revelation but I must assure you that there are only two 'End-Days' teachings which are essential to every new convert and that is these last two foundations: *"resurrection of the dead, and of eternal judgment."* Again, if you do not understand the book of Revelation, that is fine. I am glad that at the beginning of Revelation it says, *"Blessed is he that readeth, and they that hear the words of this prophecy, and keep those things which are written therein"* (1:3). In other words, you do not have to understand it all, although I would encourage you to understand it, but by simply reading it you will be blessed. You do not have to know who is who, or what is what, but this one thing you must know: I love Jesus Christ and the one thing I do know about the book of Revelation is that it is a revelation (singular, not revelations) of Jesus Christ.

The word Revelation in Greek is *apokalupsis* [from this we get our word apocalypse] which means 'to take the cover off.' It is the revealing of the person of Christ by removing the cover. True 'End-Days' teaching reveals Christ; it takes the cover off of Him. That is what this book does. It reveals the person of Christ; it unveils Him. In theology the last years of world history as prophesied in the Bible are called eschatology. But if the teaching is accurate it will be Christ-centred. So when folk talk to you of 'End-Days' and only talk about Antichrist, tribulation and great judgments on the Earth but do not reveal Christ, then you will know that that is not a complete or accurate portrayal of the biblical teaching on 'End-Days.'

There is a strong movement in the contemporary Church to avoid two topics in preaching:
1) **Repentance** and
2) **Eternal Judgment**, Hell and what happens after death on the Day of Judgment.

At best, today's Church does not say much about the latter. They are afraid to scare sinners off with negative things like sin and repentance, but here in our studies we have seen that these are indeed the foundational things, they are the milk of God's Word, not the meat. For a new Christian and as a Christian these are the only two fundamental 'End-Days' teachings which you need to be established in. If you do not know who the Antichrist is, that is not going to affect your walk with Jesus Christ. However, if you hold doubts concerning the resurrection of the dead and if they are not dealt with, they could ship-wreck your faith. It is a fundamental doctrine.

In the same way with Eternal Judgment and Hell, which we will look at in the next chapter, it is vital that every new believer be established in this teaching. Every new convert in the early Church was taught these truths and grounded in the fact that there is a resurrection and an Eternal judgment.

The Bible reveals two distinct appointments that all men will face after they die:
- resurrection of the dead,
- eternal judgment.

Before there can be a judgement in the body, there must be a resurrection of the body. You cannot be judged in the body if your body is in the grave. The resurrection of the dead comes before the Great Judgment, so we cannot talk about the Judgment without speaking first about the 'Resurrection'.

II Corinthians 5:10, *"For we must **all** appear before the judgment seat of Christ; that every one may receive the **things done in his body**, according to that he hath done, whether it be good or bad."* The word 'all' means that all Christians will appear before the judgment seat of Christ. The judgement seat of Christ is only for saints not sinners. But all of us are going to be resurrected to stand in the judgement. **Hebrews 9:27** *"And as it is appointed unto men once to die, but after this the judgment."* So the order is very clear: we die; we are resurrected; and then we appear before the judgment seat.

Note that Paul says: *"that every one may receive the **things done in his body**."* Nothing in Scripture is accidental. Every word is carefully weighed. We are told in Scripture that if all the things were written down that Christ had said and done, that all the books in the world could not contain them (Jn.21:25). This means that the Bible is the most condensed book in the world, which makes every little phrase ever more vital. The Holy Spirit cannot make mistakes! So, it specifically says that we are going to be judged for how we have lived our lives in our physical bodies. We will stand accountable and responsible for how we have lived our life: whether it be good or bad. One day your Christian life will be judged concerning how you have lived. Everything you are doing at the moment will be judged. Every thought, every word, every action, your character, your attitude—all of this one day will be revealed, exposed and opened up to judgment.

That is why around the Lord's Table every week, we read what Paul wrote to the Corinthians, *"But let a man examine himself, and so let him eat of that bread, and drink of that cup...For if we would judge ourselves, we should not be judged. But when we are judged, we are chastened of the Lord, that we should not be condemned with the world"* (I Cor.11:28, 31-32). This is a call to judge yourself. If you do not, then God will judge you. That is not a judgement unto an Eternal Hell as he makes clear in this passage. It is God dealing with us as sons, chastening us. This judging and dealing of us is to stop us being condemned with the world, which is a final judgment for sin.

Mankind is made up of: **Body, Spirit, and Soul**

1. **Body:** When you die your body will go into the grave. It is just a shell. When that body dies, the person has departed. Solomon in **Ecclesiastes 12:7** says, *"Then shall the dust return to the earth as it was:"* You are made of dust and you will return to dust. So there is a day, if you die before Christ returns, that your body will go down into a grave and be covered with soil, but you will not be there. All the body is at that point is an empty shell: a house that you have used for a short period of time.

2. **Spirit:** **Ecclesiastes 3:21** *"...the spirit of man that goeth upward."* So when there is a separation between body and spirit, the spirit will go upward. **Every** man's spirit will go up to God. **12:7** *"...the spirit shall return unto God who gave it..."* God gives to every man a spirit. It is the most inward part of man. When Adam sinned in the garden his spirit died. But in regeneration (the born-again experience) we receive a new enlivened spirit *"...a new spirit will I put within you"* (Eze.36:26). *"For thou wilt light my candle: the LORD my God will*

enlighten my darkness" (Ps.18:28). Your spirit when enlivened by the Holy Spirit is that part of you that is conscious of the things of God. **Proverbs 20:27** *"The spirit of man is the candle of the LORD, searching all the inward parts of the belly."* When a man is born again, the Spirit of God causes that candle to burst into flame. The Holy Spirit then comes to dwell in man's spirit. The Holy Spirit then enlivens you through a renewed spirit.

3. **Soul:** The soul of man is distinct from the spirit. The soul is the intellect (mind), emotions (feelings), and will (choice). The five senses of your body feed your soul. The soul is your personality or temperament. That soul makes you who you are. Choices are made in the soul realm. Just as our bodies are utterly diverse or different, so our souls are diverse. Whether you are an extravert or an introvert is directed by your soul. At the point of death the eternal soul will either go straight to Heaven or to Hell to await the resurrection.

In one sentence in Genesis, we see this tri-part creation: **Genesis 2:7,** *"And the LORD God formed man of the <u>dust of the ground</u>* [the body]*, and breathed into his nostrils the <u>breath of life</u>* [spirit]*; and man became <u>a living soul</u>* [soul]. *"*

So we see that God created the physical body first with His hands. God took soil and moulded a physical body. He formed the first man, Adam, from the dust of the Earth.

Then, secondly, God *"...breathed into his nostrils the <u>breath of life.</u>"* Now that phrase, *'breath of life'* is used in Job twice concerning the breath (Spirit) of God: **Job 27:3,** *"All the while my breath is in me, and the spirit of God is in my nostrils;"* and in **Job 33:4,** *"The Spirit of God hath made me, and the breath of the Almighty hath given me life."* So what does the Bible mean by a man's spirit or the spirit of man? It is literally the breath of God that makes man a living creature. It is God giving a man breath. The difference between a living person and a dead person is that spirit. The very second that that spirit leaves a person's body, they are dead.

Animals have a soul and if you have ever had a pet dog you

will know that they have a personality. I once had a dog that used to go in a 'huff' every single Sunday morning. It hated Sunday's because we were out for the day. It did not even lift its head when we came in or went out. It just lifted its eyes as if to say, "I know where you are going. You are leaving me all day and you won't be paying me any attention." Dogs have a personality! There is a soul within an animal, but there is not an eternal spirit. Animals do not have a consciousness of God. No animal on the face of the Earth worships God or makes an altar of prayer. You will not see an animal bow its knee to the Living God. But God *breathed* into Adam.

Thirdly, this scripture says, *"man became a living soul"*. This is where the soul comes from: when the spirit meets the body: that is when you get a personality or when your soul is created.

The soul and spirit can seem so similar and can be so hard to distinguish one from the other that it takes the sword of God's Word to divide and distinguish between them. *"For the word of God is quick, and powerful, and sharper than any twoedged sword, piercing even to the dividing asunder of soul and spirit and of the joints and marrow, and is a discerner of the thoughts and intents of the heart."* (Heb 4:12). It can be hard to discern what is coming from my renewed, regenerated spirit and what is coming from my soul but the Word of God gives us this ability.

Paul makes a very clear distinction between these three parts, in I Thessalonians 5:23, he says, *"...I pray God your whole spirit and soul and body* [he names all three] *be preserved blameless unto the coming of our Lord Jesus Christ."* Paul prays for all three 'sectors' because each one is important. The Bible says that there are sins of the body (e.g.: fornication), sins of the soul and there are sins of the spirit which is why Paul prays for each one of these three realms (I Cor.6:18; II Cor.7:1; I Pet.1:22; 2:11). Just before this he prays, *"And the very God of peace sanctify you wholly..."* In other words to be holy in all three realms—body, soul and spirit—all three must be holy. Do not think that your body does not matter. All three areas are to be sanctified as we look for the coming of Jesus. At death, the body and the soul have two different destinations. The body goes into the ground. The Spirit returns to God. The soul will either go to

Heaven or Hell.[9]

Acts 24:15, *"...there shall be a resurrection of the dead, both of the just and unjust."* Death is not a friend of mine but resurrection is. Death is not easily embraced. Death is not a thing to be desired, but there is something beyond death that is to be embraced and that ought to bring great hope, joy, and expectation to our heart. There is no hope in death but beyond death there is a hope for those who know Jesus Christ. There is a glorious hope of what awaits us after death for it shall bring us into contact with the living Christ.

"...both of the just and unjust..." So it is not only the Christian who is resurrected. Every criminal, every wicked man—even Hitler—will be resurrected one day because God says, "I want you to come back in your body and you will stand before me and I am going to judge you for every word, deed and action. You will be held accountable before me." The Bible makes it clear that, *"every one of us shall give account of himself to God,"* and that *"every knee shall bow to me, and every tongue shall confess to God"* (Rom.14:11-12). In the judgment everyone will have a knee to bend and a tongue to confess. Again, both the wicked and the just will be resurrected. Christ is going to raise them up for the purpose of the Judgment. We will all physically stand before God and be held accountable for our whole life, whether a short life or a long life. Life is very short in the light of Eternity. None of us can hold on to the sands of time. My granddad always said, "Time waits for no man." Time is moving faster than we would want it to. We would like to stop time at some points, but that is not possible.

At death the body and the soul have two different destinations. For the believer their body goes in the grave but their soul immediately goes into the presence of God. *"To be absent from the body* [is] *to be present with the Lord"* (II Cor.5:8). At the resurrection the body will be reunited with the soul. The minute I leave this body I will be in the presence of God. There is no 'soul sleep' or unconscious middle state. You are immediately in the presence of God: that is where my soul

---

[9] The eternal destination of the soul at the point of death is dealt with in the next chapter.

goes but my body will be sleeping in the Earth until the resurrection.

THERE ARE TWO DISTINCT RESURRECTIONS

Christ, in **John 5:29 says**, *"And shall come forth; they that have done good, unto the resurrection of life; and they that have done evil, unto the resurrection of damnation."* There is a resurrection of life and a resurrection of damnation. There is a resurrection for those who 'did evil' and there is a resurrection for those who 'did good'. In other words, 'doing evil' or 'doing good' separates you. A man who lives 'evil' will be separated at the point of death from the man who lives 'good'. The first will await a resurrection of damnation and the second will await a resurrection of life. The first will be given Eternal damnation and the second will be given Eternal life. It can only be one or the other. There are only two places one can spend Eternity. Every man, every woman, every boy, every girl, every person is going to spend all of Eternity in one of these two places. There will never be an end to that. It will be everlasting. So the resurrection either means life or damnation. Some people will not want to be resurrected because it will mean utter damnation. If you reject Christ in this life, He will reject you in the life to come. However, if you receive Him and bow the knee to Him in this lifetime, then He will reward you in Eternity.

We see these two resurrections again in Daniel 12:2-3, *"And many of them that sleep* [Biblical term for death] *in the dust of the earth shall awake* [be resurrected], *some to everlasting life, and some to shame and everlasting contempt. And they that be wise shall shine as the brightness of the firmament; and they that turn many to righteousness as the stars for ever and ever."*

The word resurrection means to be revived or to be raised up from the dead. Nobody was ever resurrected who was not first dead. It is the difference between a dead man and a living man. Resurrection is the supernatural power of God, raising up a body so that he who was once dead can live again.

Note, from this passage in Daniel, that it is not your soul that lies in the dust but your body. The body lies in the dust but the soul is immediately in the presence of God. Neither is it your spirit that lies in the dust because your spirit goes back to the Lord.

So again we see that there will be two separate and distinct resurrections: a resurrection of *life* and a resurrection of *contempt:* "...*some to everlasting life, and some to shame and everlasting contempt.*"

The lost are already in a conscious Hell; they are already suffering but their bodies will be resurrected out of the ground; they will be raised up to be judged at the throne of God following which they will be cast forth into everlasting contempt. So the resurrection separates utterly and eternally between the good and the evil.

There is a reward for those who experience the resurrection of the just. It says they are going to 'shine' which tells us that we are not going to be the same. When this physical body, that was lying in the dust gets raised up, when it awakens, it is going to shine like the stars of the Heaven. Those who serve Christ are going to shine as the very stars! Think of the grandeur of the stars of Heaven which we can see that twinkle and shine—we are going to shine like that! "...*they that be wise shall shine...*" Who are those wise? "*He that winneth souls is wise*" (Proverbs 11:30). He that listens to the Word of God is wise. He that builds his house on the foundation of Christ is wise. These are they who will shine.

CHRIST'S RESURRECTION

May I remind you that if we do not understand this doctrine, we will not understand many other things in Scripture. We must be established in this foundational doctrine. We must study all that the Bible has to teach us on this subject and there is no better place to start than the beautiful chapter of **I Corinthians 15,** all of which concerns the *Resurrection.*

I Cor.15:3-4, "*For I delivered unto you first of all that which I also received, how that Christ died for our sins according to the scriptures; And that he was buried, and that he rose again the third day according to the scriptures:*"

According to **verse 4,** Christ was resurrected on the third day. More than twenty times, as recorded in the Gospels, Christ declared that on the third day His Father would raise Him up from the dead. Very precisely Christ declared that after they crucified Him, after they buried Him, He would be resurrected. That is how solid the Gospel is. The Disciples who later wrote about this admit that they did not understand what He meant when He gave such clear warning about His death and then the promise of His resurrection. They could not fathom the depths of it until after He had risen from the dead. When He was crucified they got scattered abroad. They were discouraged, disheartened, and almost lost hope because His body was in the grave. They forgot that He had said time and time again that He would rise from the dead. Think about it: Christ was staking all of His ministry, all the preaching, all the miracles, all the prophecies and all of His promises upon His resurrection.

If He did not rise on the third day then everything that He said was a lie; it would be proved false. Everything depended on the Resurrection. If you remove the Resurrection, we have no Christianity. If you do not believe in the resurrection, you are not a Christian. You must believe that Christ was physically raised from the dead.

Note that all through this passage, Paul says *"according to the scriptures:"* Christ died *according to the scriptures*; He rose again, *according to the scriptures.* The Bible is our solid foundation. I know what I know because of the Scriptures. *What saith the Scriptures?* If anyone comes out with an opinion we should ask, "Where do you find that in the Scriptures?"

Paul built everything upon the Scriptures. Yes, the Spirit of God witnesses that Christ has risen from the dead but I have something more solid than that, 'Scripture says it.' Christ prophesied His resurrection and every prophecy depended on that one thing. He walked along, preaching and teaching that He would rise on the third day.

In verses 5-8, Paul then gives witnesses of that Resurrection. **v5-8,** *"And that he was seen of Cephas* [another name for Peter]*, then of the twelve: After that, he was seen of above five hundred brethren* [those in Christ] *at once; of whom the greater part remain unto this present, but some are fallen* *asleep. After that, he was seen of James; then of all the apostles. And last of all he was seen of me also, as of one born out of due time.*" This is indeed a wonderful roll-call of first-hand witnesses to the physical resurrection of Jesus Christ.

The Great Host of witnesses to the Resurrection:
- Cephas (Peter)
- The 12 Disciples
- 'Above' or over 500 Christians 'at once', meaning they were together (on the mountain side)
- James
- All the Apostles again
- Paul himself
- The Four Gospels – two of the writers were personal eye witnesses but all four drew on the personal testimonies of numerous eye witnesses.
- Acts 1:3, "*he shewed himself alive after his passion by many **infallible** proofs, being seen of them forty days.*"
- Mt.27:52-53, "*And the graves were opened; and many bodies of the saints which slept arose, And came out of the graves after his resurrection, and went into the holy city, and appeared unto many.*"
- Mary Magdalene Jn.20:14-18; Mk.16:9
- Other women, Mt.28:9
- Two on the road to Emmaus Lk.24:15

Do you remember when Christ first appeared to ten of the twelve Disciples when Thomas was not there. Thomas said, "*Except I shall see in his hands the print of the nails, and put my finger into the print of the nails, and thrust my hand into his side, I will not believe.*" We know that Christ then appeared one week later when Thomas was with the others and said unto him, "*Reach hither thy finger, and behold my hands; and reach hither thy hand, and thrust it into my side: and be not faithless, but believing...blessed are they that have not seen, and yet have believed.*" And then Christ performed "*many other signs...in the presence of his disciples*" (Jn.20:26-30). So Thomas, a righteous man, an apostle, a disciple, could not believe naturally until it was proven to him. All this to say: these were REAL witnesses to Christ's resurrected body—even Thomas doubted, but became a living witness. Imagine for all those years after Christ ascended Thomas could say, "I had doubts. I couldn't believe but then I saw Him, and I felt Him and now I am a witness that Jesus Christ was physically raised from the dead."

Note: the *"...greater part* [of 500] *remain unto this present, but some are fallen asleep."* Paul reminds the reader that there were around 500 Christians still alive who could prove that what he was writing in this Epistle, concerning the resurrection, was true. They had been there at the same time, in the same place, seeing the same resurrected Christ. Paul was inviting the reader to test what it was he was saying as those witnesses would testify to having seen Christ alive. He also notes that, *"some are fallen asleep";* in other words some of these eye witnesses had already died.

There is more written about Christ's life, death and resurrection than any other character of Ancient History. **There is far more evidence to prove that Christ lived, died and rose again, than there is to prove that Julius Caesar, or any of the great empire rulers, or leaders throughout all of ancient history, lived.** Did any of your teachers at school give you any reason to believe that they doubted the existence of Julius Caesar? No, and yet they mock those who believe in Christ! They mock the historic reality of Christ that He lived, died, and rose again even though there is an overwhelming amount of evidence.

Four books (the four gospels) write in detail on His resurrection. If the resurrection is not true then our faith is in 'vain' and Christianity is not true.

The four gospel accounts which are filled with eye-witness accounts of Christ's resurrection would easily stand up in a modern court of law. Many have set out to try and disprove the reality and truth of Christ's life and resurrection but have ended up being converted. Josh McDowell is a good example. As an intellectual man and an utter sceptic, Josh McDowell set out to disprove Christ and His Resurrection, but instead was converted and wrote a powerful book, *Evidence that Demands a Verdict*, which lays out the irrefutable evidence for Christ: His life, death, and resurrection.

Acts 1:3 *"To whom also he* [Christ] *shewed himself alive after his passion by many infallible proofs, being seen of them forty days, and speaking of the things pertaining to the kingdom of God:"*

We are reminded in this Scripture that Christ walked on Earth for **40 days** after His resurrection. For 40 days He showed them infallible proofs. The word *"infallible"* is a legal term and means proof beyond doubt; indisputable; miracles which no man could gainsay or dispute. Men could not say that it was 'psychological', 'mystical', 'just spiritual' or 'that it was the lighting', or 'a good deception' or something else. But He gave them indisputable evidence. Today the Holy Spirit does this: the Holy Spirit removes all doubt. If you have even a shade of a doubt concerning this, the Holy Spirit will convince you beyond doubt. HE has not changed.

For 40 days, Christ came and went and even ate fish and bread, which means that He had a physical, resurrected body. His body bore the marks of His death and suffering. In the book of Revelation, it says, *"And I beheld, and, lo, in the midst of the throne and of the four beasts, and in the midst of the elders, stood a Lamb as it had been slain..."* (5:6). Talking about the return of Christ, John tells us here that Christ will bear all the marks of crucifixion, but in a glorified body.

Matthew 27:52, *"And the graves were opened; and many bodies of the saints which slept* [again used for bodies lying in the grave] *arose, And came out of the graves after his resurrection, and went into the holy city, and appeared unto many."* So, shortly after Christ had risen from the dead, these folk rose up from their graves and walked into town. Can you imagine this? These 'Old Dispensation' saints would have been dead maybe a few days or maybe a few months, yet they walked into Jerusalem in their corruptible, but living bodies. Imagine the shock of friends and family as they saw the very person whom they had buried hours, days, weeks, or months before. Imagine their comments: "But you were dead! I felt your cold body. I placed you in a tomb outside the city. What are you doing here?" The answer given by these walking, living testimonies to God's resurrection power would have been, "We are here because of Christ. All He said was true. All that He claimed to be is true and we are here because HE has risen from the dead!" Resurrection is a real, historic fact!

I Cor.15:12-14, *"Now if Christ be preached that he rose from the dead, how say some among you that there is no resurrection of the dead? But if there be no resurrection of the dead, then is Christ not risen: And if Christ be not risen, then is our preaching vain, and your faith is also vain."*

Note here that we are told *"some among you"* deny the resurrection and Paul is asking them why they deny the resurrection when there are so many witnesses? There is nothing new today. There are still men and women in churches calling themselves Christians who deny the resurrection of Christ.

The Sadducees, who were 'sad you see', denied that there was a physical, literal resurrection, and did not believe in an 'After-Life'. The Sadducees denied the supernatural in the Gospel; they denied the supernatural in the Old Testament'— they did not believe that Jonah was swallowed by a big fish; they did not believe that Moses brought Israel out of Egypt and through the Red Sea with great miracles. They were probably the first Evolutionists as well.

Paul makes it clear to these, *"some among you"*, that if Christ was not raised, then faith in Christ is in vain; all preaching is in vain; to be *"vain"* means to be empty and without any weight whatsoever. There is no Christianity without the resurrection. There is no point in believing in God if you do not believe in the resurrection. If you do not believe in the resurrection, then when you die, you believe you will just stop existing. Believing in God but not believing in the resurrection is hypocrisy and makes our faith a sham.

I Cor.15:15-20 *"Yea, and we are found false witnesses of God; because we have testified of God that he raised up Christ: whom he raised not up, if so be that the dead rise not. For if the dead rise not, then is not Christ raised: And if Christ be not raised, your faith is vain; ye are yet in your sins. Then they also which are fallen asleep in Christ are perished. If in this life only we have hope in Christ, we are of all men most miserable. But now is Christ risen from the dead, and become the firstfruits of* *them that slept."* Now Paul goes on further to say that if Christ did not physically rise from the dead then the living are still in their sins. If Christ is not risen then we are not forgiven and there is no hope, no mercy, nor changed life for you. In other words you are still sinners on your way to Hell if Christ be not raised. There would be no hope, no eternal life, and no reward beyond the grave if Christ were not raised. **But** Christ was most certainly raised from the dead!

It is the resurrection power that helps me live this life. It is the resurrection power that keeps me from the lusts of this world. It is His life in me that brings forth fruit. Paul writes to the Romans that **we are saved by believing in and confessing the resurrection. Romans 10:9-10,** *"That if thou shalt confess with thy mouth the Lord Jesus, and shalt believe in thine heart that God hath raised him from the dead, thou shalt be saved. For with the heart man believeth unto righteousness; and with the mouth confession is made unto salvation."* And, **Romans 5:9,** *"Much more then, being now justified by his blood, we shall be saved from wrath through him. For if, when we were enemies, we were reconciled to God by the death of his Son, much more, being reconciled, we shall be saved by his life."* You cannot be saved unless you really believe that Christ was raised from the dead. If Christ is not risen then He is not alive and we cannot be saved. Anyone who does not believe in the resurrection is not saved. A dead Christ cannot save you only a living one can.

Again in Romans, Paul tells us **we are made righteous or justified by the resurrection.** *"Who was delivered for our offences, and was raised again for our justification"* (4:25). When Christ was raised up it meant that God had accepted His blood sacrifice. It meant that God was satisfied with the atonement. The Father said, "I accept the sacrifice," and raised Christ from the dead. That is the witness to us that we are justified. How do you know that you can be justified? You can be justified because God raised Jesus from the dead.

In **Romans 7:4**, it says that **Christ is risen that we might bring forth fruit.** *"Wherefore, my brethren, ye also are become dead to the law by the body of Christ; that ye should be married to another, even to him who is raised from the dead, that we should bring forth fruit unto God."* He is alive right now. I

114

would not be able to bring forth any Christian fruit if He were not alive. Christ's life in me makes me 'live godly'. Christ's life in me makes me leave the world. It is being joined to a resurrected Christ that brings fruit into this life. We are not following a theory or theology; Christ is alive to me and in me.

Because of the resurrection, there is no more condemnation: Romans 8:34, *"Who is he that condemneth? It is Christ that died, yea rather, that is risen again, who is even at the right hand of God, who also maketh intercession for us."* We have a man who has risen from the dead at the right hand of the Father, who ever makes intercession for us. Christ prays for each one of us all day and night. There is never a day, nor an hour when Christ is not praying for you. He is praying that you will come through trials. He is praying that you will uphold under temptation. He knows your every burden and situation and He prays for you. What a wonderful Saviour!

THE 'ORDER' OF THREE RESURRECTIONS

I Cor.15:22-24 *"For as in Adam all die, even so in Christ shall all be made alive. But every man in his own <u>order</u>: Christ the <u>firstfruits</u>; <u>afterward</u> they that are Christ's at his coming. <u>Then</u> cometh the end, when he shall have delivered up the kingdom to God, even the Father; when he shall have put down all rule and all authority and power."* Paul here speaks of an *"order"* in the resurrection which means a set order or a series in succession.

1. Christ is the *'**first fruits**'.* Christ was the first to be raised incorruptible. One day we will breathe our last breath; the death sweat will drip down our brow, but how glorious to know we can be raised like Christ was raised. The resurrection of Christ was the prototype.

2. *'**afterward**':* They that are Christ's will rise from the dead at His coming. This resurrection is for those who are born-again. When are our bodies going to be raised up from the grave? When is Mr Spurgeon going to be raised up? When are Mr Nicholson and Mr Wigglesworth going to be raised up, and all the millions of saints gone before us? At the Coming of Jesus Christ

when He returns physically and visibly to the Mount of Olives.

3. **_'Then cometh the end'_:** This comes at the end of the Millennium, at the end of Christ's 1,000 year physical reign on Earth, during which He has subdued every enemy, and at the end of which He then delivers the Kingdom back to His Father which He had received at His return to the Mount of Olives. This is when the wicked are raised and the last judgement takes place.

The Resurrection of the Righteous—living and dead
Speaking of the 'Coming of The Lord', Paul writes to the Thessalonians, *"But I would not have you to be ignorant, brethren, concerning them which are asleep,* [those who are dead in Christ] *that ye sorrow not, even as others which have no hope. For if we believe that Jesus died and rose again, even so them also which sleep in Jesus will God bring with him. For this we say unto you by the word of the Lord, that we which are alive and remain unto the coming of the Lord shall not prevent them which are asleep. For the Lord himself shall descend from heaven with a shout, with the voice of the archangel, and with the trump of God: and the dead in Christ shall rise first: Then we which are alive and remain shall be caught up together with them in the clouds, to meet the Lord in the air: and so shall we ever be with the Lord. Wherefore comfort one another with these words"* **(I Thess.4:13-18).**

In both letters to the Thessalonians, Paul mentions in every chapter the 'Return of the Lord'. They were looking for the coming of the Lord. They were a people living with that expectation of being caught up to be with Christ. They would greet one another, "Good morning, brother, Maranatha!" Their cry was, "Maranatha! Come Lord Jesus." But a change came as some started to spiritualize the promise and the prophecy concerning His return, saying that Christ's return, His coming, was past. Others took the other extreme and sold their property, gave up their jobs and literally waited out on the hillside outside Thessalonica for Christ's immediate return. This is why Paul had to tell them that if a man does not work he should not eat. Paul had to try and balance all this.

In the midst of this, Paul had to answer the question of those who wondered what had, or would, happen to their deceased loved ones. These had thought that everyone would be caught up in the Rapture before they had to taste death. So Paul comforts them with these words: *"For if we believe that Jesus died and rose again, even so them also which sleep in Jesus will God bring with him. For this we say unto you by the word of the Lord, that we which are alive and remain unto the coming of the Lord shall not prevent them which are asleep."* In other words, the Lord is going to bring those (saved ones) who have died, with Him when He returns. The Living will be 'caught up' in the air together with those who have passed before. There will be a resurrection of the dead to meet the living in the air: what a reunion! So if you pass on before me, and the Rapture takes place whilst I am still living here on Earth, then we will meet not in Heaven, not on Earth, but in the air!

(v16) *"For the Lord himself shall descend from heaven with a shout, with the voice of the archangel, and with the trump of God: and the dead in Christ shall rise first:"* Those who have gone on before us; who are already in the grave, shall rise first: their physical bodies are going to be raised up. (v17) *"Then we which are alive and remain shall be <u>caught up</u> together with them in the clouds, to meet the Lord in the air."* That term 'caught up' is a violent term and is used for a thief coming into a house and means, to seize or to grab. That is what the Rapture is: it is when we suddenly get grabbed, or caught away up into the air. Elsewhere we are told that we, our physical bodies, are going to be changed *"in the twinkling of an eye."* Our physical bodies will be changed to become a resurrection body, *"and so shall we ever be with the Lord. Wherefore <u>comfort one another</u> with these words."* When one of us dies, we can comfort one another by saying, "We shall see him or her again in that great gathering in the clouds."

Our resurrection is founded on Christ's resurrection. If Christ was not resurrected physically, literally and visibly, then we have no hope for our resurrection.

The Resurrection of the Wicked

Revelation 20:4-6, *"...and they* [believers] *lived and reigned with Christ a thousand year. But the rest of the dead lived not again until the thousand years were finished. <u>This is the first resurrection</u>. Blessed and holy is he that hath part in the first resurrection: on such the second death hath no power..."*

Briefly on the Millennium: Some people have tried to say that there is only one chapter in the Bible that talks about the Millennium and that it is only mentioned four times. Well, the Bible says far less about some other things that we all consider to be sure. We certainly have enough in the Bible to believe in the 1,000 year Reign of Jesus Christ. The Bible says we will reign with Jesus Christ 1,000 years, but the rest of the dead live *'not again until the thousand years were finished.'* So in new resurrection bodies, in new dominions, the saints will reign with Christ for 1,000 years, but sinners will lie in the grave and will not be raised until the end of the Millennium.

At the end of the Millennium, just before the Great Judgement, death and Hell opens up and offers up all those who are in Hell. **Rev.20:12-13,** *"And I saw the dead, small and great, stand before God; and the books were opened: and another book was opened, which is the book of life: and the dead were judged out of those things which were written in the books, according to their works. And the sea gave up the dead which were in it; and <u>death and hell delivered up the dead</u> which were in them: and they were judged every man according to their works."*

Every man, every woman, every wicked person, every atheist—all of them will return in a new physical body and will stand in the presence of God to be judged. Paul wrote to the Church at Philippi:*"That I may know him, and the power of his resurrection, and the fellowship of his sufferings, being made conformable unto his death; <u>If by any means I might attain unto the resurrection of the dead"</u>* **(3:10-11).** Why does Paul say 'IF' (*"If by any means"*) if everyone will be resurrected? Why must he *attain unto the resurrection?* Because Paul wants to attain unto the resurrection of the Righteous! He wants to 'attain' unto the resurrection of the righteous, a better resurrection, not the resurrection of the wicked. He wants to live his life in such a way that he will be a part of that first resurrection; that glorious resurrection.

The Resurrection Body
Finally, Paul addresses one last issue in **I Cor.15:35-36**: *"But some man will say, How are the dead raised up? and with what body do they come? Thou fool, that which thou sowest is not quickened, except it die."* There are those who cannot comprehend and understand how a resurrection can come out of a man's body dying, being buried and then decaying in the ground. If little remains of the body how can the same body be resurrected?

To give an answer Paul goes on to speak about the principle of the seed and the act of sowing and reaping that we see all around us. Paul calls those who get confused over this principle, *"fools"*, meaning they are not applying any thought to this and are irrational in their questions about the resurrection body and are foolish in harbouring confusion as to how their physical bodies which are laid in the grave can be resurrected as new eternal bodies. The body of a seed sown in the ground is very different from the body the seed produces in death. Death is the instrument by which the body is made alive in a new body. The body that goes into the grave is different when it comes out of the grave. One thing is sure, if you sow a wheat seed then you will get wheat back after the death of the seed. A seed produces after its kind. God has uniquely given all seeds and all things their own body as it has pleased Him.

In Creation he shows that there are different types of bodies which he calls *"flesh."* Although they are all flesh yet the flesh, or body, is different for men, beasts, fish, and birds (v39). Each of these is different yet they all have physical bodies. He also says that, *"There are also celestial bodies..."* meaning heavenly bodies, and *"bodies terrestrial"*, meaning earthly bodies (v40). Each has distinct forms of glory; all are not the same although all have a form or body. *"There is one glory of the sun, and another glory of the moon, and another glory of the stars: for one star differeth from another star in glory"* (v41).

From all of these examples he then comes to the *"resurrection of the dead"* (v42). By all of the above examples he wants to show the difference in the body we sow in the ground and the body we shall receive back at the resurrection. And so he explains this process that happens to the body:

- Sown in corruption, raised in incorruption (v42)
- Sown in dishonour, raised in glory (v43)
- Sown in weakness, raised in power
- Sown a natural body, raised a spiritual body (v44)

The body we receive at the resurrection will be radically different from our present physical body yet it will be the same recognisable body, only changed. We will know one another and I am certain that we shall carry similar likenesses, yet in a body that is eternal without any form of decay, with great glory and power. It will be a spiritual body yet a body that will still have flesh and bones (Lk.24:3).

Paul finishes his teaching on a wonderful high note just as we shall. **I Cor.15:52-55,** *"In a moment, in the twinkling of an eye, at the last trump: for the trumpet shall sound, and the dead shall be raised incorruptible, and we shall be changed. For this corruptible must put on incorruption, and this mortal must put on immortality. So when this corruptible shall have put on incorruption, and this mortal shall have put on immortality, then shall be brought to pass the saying that is written, Death is swallowed up in victory. O death, where is thy sting? O grave, where is thy victory?"*

CHAPTER 7

ETERNAL JUDGMENT

There are times when the joy of the LORD ought to grip our hearts and make us dance for joy, but then there are times when we must sit down and be sober. There are some truths of the Bible which bring great lightness and joy to our hearts, like the last chapter when we looked at the Resurrection, but then there are some truths which are weighty and bring great seriousness, sobriety, and solemnity. Eternal judgment is of the latter kind. There are some things that are not meant to be laughed about. There are some truths which are meant to sober you up and to make you sit down and consider deeply. If looking into Eternity and knowing that there is an everlasting judgment does not sober you up, then nothing this side of Eternity will. We ought to be preparing and making ourselves ready for our eternal destiny. We—every man, woman, young and old; out of every generation and nation—have an appointment to keep with God in Eternity. May God open the eyes of our hearts that we might see in such a way that it would affect our walk.

Hebrews 6:2b *"... and of resurrection of the dead, and of eternal judgment."* Remember we said in the previous chapter that many talk about the 'Last Days' or 'End Days' and want to know about 'End Day events' or the Antichrist and suchlike, but the Bible teaches that there are only two essential teachings concerning 'End Days' and these are the two foundations of, *'resurrection of the dead, and of eternal judgment'*. We must be gripped with these truths and have a fundamental understanding of them. These truths ought to bring joy to our hearts and seriousness in our walk with God.

Eternal Judgment is not a popular topic but every babe in Christ, every new convert needs to know all about it. Every new believer that walks through the doors of our churches needs to hear and know about Eternal Judgment. This is not a topic restricted to the mature or those who know the depths of Christ. This is the milk of the Word. Eternal Judgment is an 'ABC'. You cannot know Christ, walk with Christ, or understand Christ in any depth, unless you understand Eternal Judgment. You cannot grow to maturity in the person of Christ without first understanding that He is a judge and that He will judge the World.

Hebrews 10:30, tells us that, *"The Lord shall judge his people."* So the Lord shall judge believers—not just sinners. This is a certainty: Christ will judge the Church. God is going to judge you, me, every Christian, every believer, not just the world out there, not just sinners. God is going to judge your life and my life. There is a day when the Lord is going to judge us.

But he goes further in **Hebrews 12:22-23**, *"God the Judge of all..."* when he says *"all"* he means all men. **Heb.13:4**, *"...whoremongers and adulterers God will judge."* This reiterates that everybody is going to be judged by Christ.

Some people think (incorrectly) that because Christ suffered on the Cross for our sins, died for our sins and was judged for our sins, that we will not be judged in the future. But Christ died for our sins *in time*, not in Eternity. The judgment spoken of here is not past judgment (at Calvary), but future judgment. Future, or eternal judgment is that judgment which will take place in Eternity after Christ comes. Eternal Judgment is that appointment in Eternity when you will stand before Christ so that He can judge you.

We know the day of our salvation. We know that there was a day and a time when we met the man of Calvary, when He washed away our sins and cleansed us, but there is another day which we must know is coming no matter how perfect or sinless you are! The Christ who bled and suffered for you, will one day stand before you and judge your life.

Heb.12:29, *"For our God is a consuming fire."* We must remember that God is love: He is indeed merciful and gracious, but He is also holy, He is *a consuming fire*. God burns as a fire: that is His nature and character and that is why if you saw Him now, you would die physically. There is something unbelievably awesome about our God that we can hardly fathom.

Jude 1:14-15, *"And Enoch also, the seventh from Adam, prophesied...saying, Behold, the Lord cometh with ten thousands of his saints, To execute judgment upon all..."* Note that Enoch was the seventh generation or the seventh in line so this was a very early stage after Creation in recorded history. This passage records Enoch prophesying that *'the Lord cometh with ten thousands of his saints, To execute judgment upon all.'* Enoch, the man who walked with God and who was 'raptured', had such intimate fellowship with the Lord, that the Lord shared His heart with him. Out walking one day, they were in such close communion that the Lord said, 'Well, we are closer to my home than yours, so come on home with me.' Enoch is one of only two men who never died physically but in the days when he walked this Earth, he prophesied, *"the Lord cometh with ten thousands of his saints, To execute judgment upon all."* This prophecy speaks of Christ returning with all of His people.

If you had bumped into Enoch on the road, he would have warned you of that coming judgment, the prospect of which made Enoch walk with God. We see then that from the beginning of recorded history, there was a warning from those who walked with God of a coming day of judgment. From Genesis to Revelation—every book—there is a warning of this coming judgment, that our God is a Holy God and righteous judge.

We know that God judged (and judges) in physical time. For example we can read of Korah and the Rebellion (Numbers 16). Korah rejected God-appointed authority; he rejected Moses and he rejected Aaron. Korah rose up and said, 'Sure, we can all lead. We are all appointed to lead. Who is Moses? Who is Aaron?' Well, God opened up the ground itself and Korah literally fell into Hell—body and soul. This is the first and only incident of this happening in the Bible. That was *judgment in time* not Eternity.

A second example of *judgment in time* is the king of Israel, Herod (Acts 12:21-25). As he gave an oration we are told that the people shouted out, *"It is the voice of a god, and not of a man."* Because Herod received such praise and did not give God the glory an angel smote him and he was eaten of worms and died.

A third example is Ananias and Sapphira. This couple attended a church that was caught up in revival yet they lied in giving the impression that they had given all of the money they made on the sale of land to the Lord. They lied to the Holy Ghost so God judged them. That is not Eternal Judgment, that is *judgment in time* and I can assure you that the judgment of Ananias and Sapphira is nothing in comparison to that coming Day of Judgment. Think about it: God said, "A lie is so bad that I am going to kill you in church in the midst of my people." This ought to make us fear that day which is coming. We had better tremble at the thought of that day. Anyone who tells you that you have nothing to worry about concerning that day is misleading you. You ought to fear that day. This is not fear of rejection but fear that you will be held accountable for your Christian life.

Daniel 7:9-10, *"...the Ancient of days* [Christ] *did sit...his throne was like the fiery flame, and his wheels as burning fire. A fiery stream issued and came forth from before him...the judgment was set, and the books were opened."* Daniel is here preaching about the last judgment. This describes how Christ is going to be seated. The books are going to be opened and Christ will be ready to judge.

Acts 17:31, "[God] *hath appointed a day, in the which he will judge the world in righteousness by that man whom he hath ordained."* The 'man' mentioned here is Christ. The Christ we love and the Christ we remember every Lord's Day is the Christ who is literally coming as the Judge.

Jesus—yesterday rejected, today mocked and scorned, but on that day Jesus will sit as a king with full sovereign power to judge the whole earth. Nobody will be laughing at Him then. Nobody will mock Him. There is a day coming when He will sit as a judge. On that day He will put everything right. He will turn everything the right way up. He will judge every heart and every man will be held accountable for how he has lived. Just think, the wickedness of our nations, the immorality, the abuse of children, the murder and atrocities committed, not one man shall 'get away' or escape the consequence thereof.

Some think that if someone kills 50 people, then commits suicide, that they have escaped judgment. Oh, no! They have not escaped at all! There is a day appointed for their judgment. The world did not have an opportunity to judge Hitler because he committed suicide, but there is a day of judgment coming. Life works out righteously in the end. For those in the world, this lifetime is not fair. There is no justice in this lifetime. Things do not work out right. But for the believer everything will work out right and fair in the end! Family members may laugh and scorn at you but one day all of this will be set in righteous order. This world can laugh at us, they can reject and stone us but one day that will be put right. For the believer there is justice and righteousness because there will be a day of judgment when everything is put right.

What the words 'judge' and 'judgment' mean

The word judge or judgment means, 'to distinguish, to try, determine, decide, conclude, or decree'. So Christ will 'try' your life. He will separate things out in your life. He will scrutinize and divide things out. He will decide, conclude, and decree. He will sift through our lives, separating the good from the bad; the real from the false; hypocrisy and sham from reality and transparency. In this lifetime we do not see that. But God's judgment is going to scrutinize every motive, every thought, and every action.

The angels presently look at the wheat and tares growing together and they ask God if they can go in there and sort out the confused mixture that seems to be in the kingdom of God but God tells them to wait until the harvest time which is the end of the world when God will separate the wheat from the tares, the goats from the sheep, and the righteous from the wicked by judging men (Mt.13:24-30).

This word *"judgment"* is the Greek word *Bema* and was taken from the Grecian games. It was a podium where successful athletes were rewarded for victory in athletic contests. Every Greek person or at least those families in Greek culture would fully understand exactly what a *Bema* was. It can be used in four different ways:

    i)   A podium to speak from: an elevated area where a man would go to speak or to make a pronouncement.

    ii)   A place of judgment and trial: if you caused a brawl you would be brought to the Bema and your case judged. (There were Bema seats in Corinth, Athens, and Jerusalem). It would be like us using the term, 'courthouse'.

iii) A measurement of the foot: to put up the length of your foot: in other words, your walk is going to be judged! How you have walked, lived, conducted yourself will come into judgment.

iv) A place of reward: (Mt.27:19; Jn.19:13; Acts 18:12, 16, 17; 25:6, 10, 17). This was the place of reward where the Olympic athlete would have received his reward. Note that to take part in the Grecian games 2,000 years ago a man would have made tremendous sacrifices. He would have separated and dedicated his life to training for the games. He would have given up alcohol and immorality for at least several months before it for the sake of the race or else he would be disqualified. These athletes moulded their whole life around the one goal of being able to stand at that *Bema* seat and receive a reward. Their whole life was lived for that day. They lived wondering whether they would be qualified for that award or whether they would be disqualified. All their training, sacrifices, and labour would be revealed on that day. All the buffeting and training, the living of a disciplined life and the bringing under of the body is worth it all on that day.

Several aspects of the coming judgment:
1. Judgment of Nations and Cities (Mt.25:31-46). Christ teaches that *"all nations"* will one day be gathered before Him in judgment. The word *"nations"* is *ethnos* where we get the word 'ethnic', meaning people group. A nation will be judged on how they responded to Him working in and through His people in that particular nation. He will separate between the sheep and goats. This is not the wholesale separation of nations as sheep or goat nations but the final separation of individuals within the nations. They will either hear *"Come, ye blessed of my Father, inherit the kingdom*

prepared for you from the foundation of the world" or *"Depart from me, ye cursed, into everlasting fire, prepared for the devil and his angel."* Christ also revealed in His preaching that cities would receive judgment according to the opportunities they had received. Cities that had experienced His miraculous ministry but rejected His message would be judged more harshly than very wicked cities that saw no miracle. The cities of Chorazin, Bethsaida and Capernaum which Christ preached in were held more accountable than these others: *"It shall be more tolerable for Tyre, Sidon and [Sodom] at the day of judgment, than for you"* (Mt.11:21-24). He says that if the *"mighty works"* (*dunamis*) which had been done in these cities had been done in cities like Sodom *"they would have repented long ago in sackcloth and ashes"* and *"would have remained until this day."* It would seem by this that those punished in *"everlasting fire"* will have different degrees of intensity in their punishment although all are eternally punished.

2. Judgment of Israel (Mt.19:38; Lk.22:30). The twelve Disciples were told by Christ, *"ye which have followed me, in the regeneration when the Son of man shall sit in the throne of his glory, ye also shall sit upon twelve thrones, judging the twelve tribes of Israel."*

3. Judgment of the Angels (I Cor.6:3) Paul, speaking to the Corinthian Church asks them *"Know ye not that we shall judge angels? how much more things that pertain to this life?"* Paul is tired of their disputes and arguments (one brother is taking another brother to the court house) and asks them is there not one wise man among them who can judge things righteously? He suggests that they choose one who is least esteemed in the church to judge this thing. Paul challenged them that they ought to be able to make judgments in life between what is right and what is wrong. He goes on to remind them that one day they will judge majestic angels full of splendour. You are a sinner redeemed by grace but you are going to judge angels one day. We are not told whether we will judge both elect and fallen angels but we can assume it is both.

4. Judgment Seat of Christ (*Bema* Seat) **Lk.14:14,** *"...for thou shalt be recompensed at the resurrection of the just."* When God resurrects the saints, those who are just, His Church, His redeemed people, they are raised up and given a new body for this purpose, so as to be able to stand in judgment. Note, this is a judgment of recompense or reward. Christ is going to reward the saints. The redeemed will stand there in a redeemed incorruptible body and will be rewarded for their lives on Earth. Christ will reward those who came out of this world and followed Him. What a glorious thought! Not only are we going to get that new incorruptible body, but we are going to get a reward. All the splendour of the Olympic Award ceremony will be nothing in comparison to that day. All the saints out of every nation, generation, and culture will be rewarded. Anyone who suffers for the faith will be rewarded. Nothing will be missed. In this lifetime we may miss out on things as a believer but God says, "I am going to pay you back in full!" You may never be rewarded in any way this side of Eternity but there is a day coming when you will be rewarded.

Rom.14:10, *"But why dost thou judge thy brother? Or why dost thou set at nought thy brother?* [to criticise, judge or make little of or have low thoughts of your brother] *for we shall **all** stand before the judgment seat of Christ."* Note that Paul includes himself. We shall all—ALL BELIEVERS—be gathered there on that day. So we see that the judgment seat of Christ is ONLY for believers or those born-again.

II Cor.5:10, *"For we must* ["must" means that there is no way around this or any exceptions to it] ***all** appear before the judgment seat of Christ; that every one may receive the things done in his body, according to that he hath done, whether it be good or **bad**."* Christ will not be judging our salvation but He will be judging our works. This is not a judgment of your sin, as that was dealt with at Calvary, and can only be dealt with this side of Eternity. He will be dealing with how you have lived your life. It is a judgment of your works. This is a judgment and reward of

128

works done in your body, not of salvation or whether or not you get into the Kingdom.

In a moment in the 'twinkling of an eye' God will gather all your atoms, your molecules—whatever makes up your physical body—and He will call you to this judgment. It does not matter if your dust and ashes have been scattered to the four corners of the Earth, your body is going to be reassembled. We are going to look the same but our bodies will be utterly perfect. We will be able to recognize each other and see the same features. Because we lived this life in the flesh, we will be judged in the flesh. We will no longer have an old flesh life or nature but we will have a body. We will not have one single attitude or thought that is wrong. We will be absolutely perfect. We will be perfected in body, soul, and mind and will stand before God without any shadow of darkness and will be free from apathy and temptation. At this point you will not be able to 'make up for anything'; it will be too late. All your lifetime as a believer will come into judgment. Not your life as a sinner but your life after you were saved, yet it says that He will sift between good and bad. Note that the word '_**bad**_' means worthless; useless; good for nothing; or of no spiritual value. God is going to search out your innermost being to discern to the depths what was useless and what was of eternal value.

I Corinthians 3:10-15, *"According to the grace of God which is given unto me, as a wise masterbuilder, I have laid the foundation, and another buildeth thereon. But let every man take heed how he buildeth thereupon. For other foundation can no man lay than that is laid, which is Jesus Christ. Now if any man build upon this foundation gold, silver, precious stones, wood, hay, stubble; Every man's work shall be made manifest: for the day shall declare it, because it shall be revealed by fire; and the fire shall try every man's work of what sort it is. If any man's work abide which he hath built thereupon, he shall receive a reward. If any man's work shall be burned, he shall suffer loss: but he himself shall be saved; yet so as by fire."*

To reiterate: This is not a judgment of the soul concerning

salvation but of works in service to Christ. It is a judgment of things done in the body, during your time on Earth, after conversion. No false converts, no game-players, no foolish virgins, and no hypocrites will appear at the Judgment seat of Christ (Bema seat). Only real, genuine believers will stand at this throne.

"...as a wise masterbuilder" God had literally given Paul a master plan so that he could build a house with Christ as its foundation. This master plan is revealed in the epistles he wrote. Those who stand at this throne on that day are only those who had Christ as their foundation in life. Your sin will not come before God on that day, but Paul warns that you had better be careful what you build on that foundation because God is going to test it. You can build with, *"gold, silver, precious stones,"* which are all found under ground level, hidden from the sight of man, whereas, *"wood, hay, stubble"* are found in plenteous supply above ground level. The former are 'precious': you have to labour and dig for them and they can also withstand fire. But wood, hay, and stubble will be easily gained but even more easily burned. Gold, silver, and precious stones increase in worth, they do not corrupt and do not fade.

God is saying that there are some things in your Christian walk which if you build them into your life will still be there in a thousand or million years' time. Wood, hay and stubble will be those things that will only affect this lifetime. They will not go into Eternity as they will burn up at the judgment. Everything in your Christian life is either in the one group or the other. Let me ask you: how much of what you have done in your Christian walk from the day you were saved will be judged as wood, hay, and stubble? God does not care for those things and they will not go into Eternity. How many things in our life are useless and of no eternal value?

Remember, our relationships as believers will go on into Eternity. The true, intimate fellowship of the saints will continue on into Eternity. Prayer meetings will not; preaching will not; but our fellowship in Christ will go straight through into Eternity. It is not how MUCH you have done for Christ, but it is a case of what type, value or quality your works are. If you only have a little bit of gold that is fine but you had better be sure that it is secure. You could have enough wood, hay, and stubble to pack out a thousand barns, but it will all burn up.

The Bible says that Christ's eyes are like flames of fire. It is those eyes that are going to thoroughly search the works of His people. He will peer into the depths of your being. How much is going to burn? How many weeks months or years of your life are going to be burnt up? Or of how much is He going to say, "This is precious. This is gold. This is silver."

Every morning we rise, we should ask, "Am I going to build gold, silver, or precious stones on that foundation today?" Every evening we should ask whether we have built with wood, hay, or stubble. Sadly, we have lost the seriousness of this appointment when our whole life will have fire burn through it.

Thomas Walsh, one of Wesley's greatest preachers who lived here in Limerick, once rebuked Mr. Wesley. He said, "Mr. Wesley, you do tempt me to lightheartedness." We would not think of John Wesley as a light-hearted man and yet Thomas Walsh did not want to be a partaker of anything light-hearted because he knew there was such a judgment coming.

WHAT WILL BE JUDGED?

Our Works will be judged:
(v 13) *"Every man's work shall be made manifest: for the day shall declare it, because it shall be revealed by fire;"* The fire shall reveal the nature of our works: *"...the fire shall try every man's work of what sort it is. If any man's work abide which he hath built thereupon, he shall receive a reward. If any man's work shall be burned, he shall suffer loss: but he himself shall be saved; yet so as by fire."* You could lose your reward but be saved. Like Lot, of whom the Bible calls, *"...just Lot..."* as well as pronouncing him a, *"righteous man"* and speaks concerning his *"righteous soul",* yet it is evident from the story of his life that he was a man saved, *'as by fire'.* He was justified by faith but built very little upon this foundation of any worth. He never did anything in service to God of eternal consequence but he got to Heaven. Saints, you do not want to get there like that! Do not 'scrape in'! Do not be satisfied just to be a true convert. Let us make our lives worth something in the Kingdom of God. Let us

not get there and find that we got there but we spent our years playing games. What are you going to do in the week to come? What are you going to do in the year to come?

Our 'works' which will be tested by fire are our service: what we do with our hands; where we go and the activities we are involved with are going to be judged.

Our Words will be judged:

Malachi tells us that the words of those who fear the Lord are going to be recorded in a book of remembrance (3:16). Is your conversation worth recording? Is your tongue set on fire by Heaven or by Hell? God keeps a book and when the saints come together God tells a heavenly scribe to start recording the conversation. Many conversations are going to cause the book to be shut. But the conversations of those who love the Lord, who tremble when they speak of Him, these will be recorded. We will never be judged for talking too much about the Lord or making too much of Him. Topics of discussion which are not necessarily sinful will not be recorded in that book. For example, God will not be recording your discussions on politics, no matter how wise sounding they are. Only conversations governed by the fear of God will be recorded.

Christ gave a very sobering warning concerning this coming judgment of our words: *"But I say unto you, That every idle word that men shall speak, they shall give account thereof in the day of judgment. For by thy words thou shalt be justified, and by thy words thou shalt be condemned"* (Mt.12:36-37; Prov.13:3). The word, *"idle,"* Christ uses here means useless or lazy. Useless, wasteful conversations will one day be judged. Those who do not set a watch over their mouth are very foolish.

Our Thoughts will be judged:

Romans 2:15-16 *"Which shew the work of the law written in their hearts, their conscience also bearing witness, and their thoughts the mean while accusing or else excusing one another;) In the day when God shall judge the secrets of men by Jesus Christ according to my gospel."* The deep things of a man's heart: his motives and his conscience will be called out to bear witness. On that Day of Judgment, your conscience will be called out to bear witness either for or against you (Rom.2:15-16). Your conscience will give evidence on that day. Your conscience will reveal much concerning the inward motive of every thought. Your conscience is God-given and it tells you 'that is right' or 'that is wrong'; 'don't do that!' or 'don't go there!' and on that day your conscience will recall how you were warned. Your conscience will be like a record-keeper or the *black box* of an aeroplane. Your *black box* will be opened up: this is the 'laying bare' of your conscience.

Just like that *black box* your conscience has a record of every conversation, every motive, every word, every action—everything is recorded. That *black box* tells the engineers every button that was turned and every action that took place on that aeroplane. In the same way, God is going to take your conscience on the Day of Judgment, open it up to make a thorough search of our every motive and every thought. Note: every motive will be scrutinized. Actions can be right but if motives are wrong the action will be burnt up. You can die without any one on Earth knowing the motive of your heart yet on that day it shall be revealed. Christ, with His eyes of fire, is going to penetrate to the motives of your heart. Why did you say that? Why did you tell that story? Why did you make that phone call? Why did you send that email? Everything is going to be scrutinized. If your motive is wrong it is wood, hay, and stubble. You may have done something with an ulterior, hidden motive—that will be searched out by fire. You could die saying 'nobody knows' or, 'nobody notices' or, 'nobody sees the motives of my heart' but on that day, everything will be revealed.

THE CROWNS

Most people say that there are five crowns but I find six. Let us look at them:

1. **The incorruptible crown**: Incorruptible meaning, it will last forever. This is the **crown of self-Denial**, death to self or self-control or it could be called the 'Runners' Crown'. It is for faithfulness in self-control. It is for a *bringing under* of that old nature. The 'runner' who brings his actions, attitude, and life

under control and is self-disciplined will receive this crown. You can be saved and say, 'I'm forgiven; I'm ok. I know I'm going to Heaven,' but you can be undisciplined, so you will be disqualified from receiving this crown. The Bible says, when we stand before Him, He is going to search and ask, 'Did you discipline yourself?' 'Did you die to your own ambitions or your own ideas?' *"Know ye not that they which run in a race run all, but one receiveth the prize? So run, that ye may obtain. And every man that striveth for the mastery is **temperate in all things**. Now they do it to obtain a corruptible crown; but we an incorruptible...I keep under my body, and bring it into subjection: lest that by any means, when I have preached to others, I myself should be a castaway"* **(I Cor.9:25)**. Will you receive this incorruptible crown which says that you disciplined yourself? On that day will it be revealed that here stands a man or woman who disciplined themselves to seek the Lord and to read His Word?

2. **The crown of rejoicing**: This is the **soul-winner's crown** or the crown for faithfulness in service. Paul writes, *"For what is our hope, or joy, or crown of rejoicing? Are not even ye in the presence of our Lord Jesus Christ at his coming?"* **(I Thess. 2:19)**. Paul had won these Thessalonians to the Lord. He had preached to them and given them the Gospel so he says that on that day they will be the rejoicing of his heart. Note though: it is not the quantity of souls that you win, but the quality. Be sure you take someone to Heaven. Samuel Rutherford, the great Scottish preacher and scholar, said if he got to Heaven and saw one soul from Anwoth (where he lived and ministered for 10 years), his Heaven would be two Heavens. Are you willing to pray a soul in? Have you won a soul to Christ who will reach Heaven?

3. **The crown of life**: This crown is given for **enduring temptation or going through trials** (Faithfulness in temptation or trial) *"Blessed is the man that endureth temptation:* [uphold under temptation] *for when he is tried, he shall receive the crown of life, which the Lord hath promised to them that love him"* (James 1:12). Some people cave in when the Devil brings a

certain temptation their way. The Devil knows your weak point whether it is your tongue, your mind, or your attitude. But God knows where to meet you in order to help you. He wants you to jump that hurdle. You may have failed last time, last month, or last year, but you can jump that hurdle this time.

Red Rum was a horse who had been put out to pasture. His owner thought that there was no future for him in racing, so he was put out to pasture to live out his days. But a trainer passed by one day and observed the horse, and offered to take *Red Rum* and train him. This reject came back from a place of obscurity to win one of the most famous races in the world. *Red Rum* became a legend as he won the *Grand National* race three times running. He became a world champion who for his great fame was buried on the finish line.

Let us run this race so that there will be rejoicing on that day. There is a real lifestyle of enduring in temptation and under trial that will be rewarded on that day with a crown.

4. **The crown of righteousness**: given **for loving His appearing**
"I have fought a good fight, I have finished my course, I have kept the faith: Henceforth there is laid up for me a crown of righteousness, which the Lord, the righteous judge, shall give me at that day: and not to me only, but unto all them also that love his appearing" (II Tim.4:8). When Paul wrote this he was sitting in a prison cell shortly before his martyrdom. This crown of righteousness is given to them who love His appearing. He defines what this crown-winning love looks like. This crown will be given to those who were faithful in fighting the fight, finishing the race and in keeping the faith. All of this is considered to be righteousness, motivated by love and rewarded by a righteous judge with a crown of righteousness. If you love Christ's Coming, you will walk faithfully in righteousness till the end.

5. **The crown of glory**: This crown is for leaders, elders or those shepherding the flock; it is the **Crown of the Under-Shepherd**. Faithfulness in tending those entrusted to you. *"And they that be wise shall shine as the brightness of the firmament; and they that turn many to righteousness as the stars for ever and ever"*

(Dan.12:3). *"The <u>elders which are among you I exhort, who am</u> <u>also an elder</u>* [Note: Peter, is gifted as an Apostle, but he is saying he too is an elder]...*Feed the flock of God which is among* *you, taking the <u>oversight</u> thereof, not by constraint, but willingly;* *not for filthy lucre* [money], *but of a ready mind; Neither as* *being <u>lords over God's heritage</u>, but being ensamples* [examples] *to the flock. And when the chief Shepherd shall appear, ye shall* *receive a crown of glory that fadeth not away"* **(I Pet.5:1-4).**

Please notice that the Greek word for God's ***heritage*** is the word *'kleros'* from which we get our modern term, 'cleric'. The terms 'cleric or clergy' today generally means one who has received religious ordination to the task of ministry that is barred to others. From this verse above we can see that all of God's people, His flock, His inheritance were once called the *'kleros'* (clergy) but today we have made a man with a funny collar the *'kleros'*. Then, as Peter used it, it meant all the people of God, but now it means the select few. Such abuse of terms gave rise to the clergy–laity divide. A caste system arose in the church which took titles, garments, honours and preferment that was utterly unlike Christ, Peter or the early church elders. We must realise that elders and gifted ministries are a part of the body of Christ like everyone else.

This crown of glory is given to faithful elders. Anyone who has abused the flock will not receive this crown. I would not want to stand on that judgment day before Christ if I knew that I had abused the flock of God. All preaching, ministry, and all counselling of the flock is going to be tested by fire. The ministry of every shepherd, preacher, and elder will be judged. The fire will test your motive for being in ministry and why you do ministry. It will test your faithfulness in your task of overseeing the flock. It will test your faithfulness in feeding the flock with the Word of God. If you have fed them with jokes, games, entertainment, fables, heresies, or spiritual junk food, it will burn up on that day.

Lastly, you will be judged on whether you walked in front of them leading them by your example or if you drove them from behind with demands that you did not live out.

It is no light thing to be in ministry. I see people fighting to be in ministry but they must know that they will be judged with a greater judgment. James wrote *"My brethren, be not many masters, knowing that we shall receive the greater condemnation"* **(3:1)**. James urged that not many should seek to be teachers because they will have a greater judgment. An Elders' judgment will be more intense, more scrutinizing than that of the sheep. You may not like other people judging your ministry now but I want to assure you that you would be well advised to judge yourself and your own ministry because it will be scrutinized inside–out at the *Bema* seat of Christ.

6. **The crown of martyrdom**: *"...be thou faithful unto death, and I will give thee a crown of life"* **(Rev.2:10)**. This is the martyr's crown. Now someone could be 'martyred' but they do not do it out of love: *"though I give my body to be burned, and have not charity, it profiteth me nothing."* (I Cor. 13:3b). It is vain, empty, or wood, hay and stubble to die as a Christian martyr but not have love. God will say it was a waste of time. Think about this: a martyr's heart motive will qualify or disqualify him from receiving this crown not just the act itself. On the contrary you could just give someone a glass of water but if you do it in the name of the Lord, with charity, you shall receive a reward. *"Blessed are they which are persecuted for righteousness' sake: for theirs is the kingdom of heaven"* **(Mt.5:10)**.

Before we move on to the question of 'Hell,' I want to remind you that the Judgment Seat of Christ (Bema seat) is for the saints of God. You will stand alone before that throne and be judged. If we kept this in mind each day upon rising and each night upon going to bed, we might walk very differently.

CHRIST & HADES

Hell has everything to do with judgment <u>for sinners</u> and so we must talk about Hell if we are going to cover everything in this subject of Eternal Judgment. Let us take a look at the different words used for 'Hell' in the Bible.

1. The first one in Hebrew is **Sheol** and it literally means, 'to demand; inquire; request; or never be satisfied'. This is a picture of Hell. Hell demands, "Give me lives! Give me

lives!" **Proverbs 27:20** says, *"Hell and destruction are never full; so the eyes of man are never satisfied."* Hell is demanding at this very moment, "Give me souls from Ireland! Give me souls out of Limerick!" I wish the Church was as demanding as Hell is. Every day, we should not be satisfied until we see souls come into the Kingdom; souls for Heaven. Where is that burning passion to see men in Heaven rather than in Hell? While Hell screams for Irish men to burn eternally in its fires, the Church sleeps and entertains itself. *Sheol* is translated as 'Hell' 31 times; as 'grave' 31 times, and 'pit' 3 times, but in all of these it is NOT talking of the physical grave where the body lies but the place a person's soul goes to at death. Distinct from this is the different Hebrew word for grave, *queber*, which always speaks of the physical grave for the body.

2. The second word for Hell is, ***Tophet***, which is also the name of the Valley of Hinnom a valley south-west of Jerusalem, where all the rubbish was burnt (Isa.30:3). At times of revival they took all the idols and burnt them in this valley. When the Hebrews thought about Hell they thought about *Tophet* where fires burned continually to get rid of the rubbish.

3. In the New Testament, Jesus talks often about, ***Hades,*** this literally means, 'unseen or hidden'. It is equivalent in meaning to *Sheol* in the Old Testament. It is used eleven times in the New Testament and Christ used it ten of those times. Note: Christ talked more about Hell than anybody else in the New Testament. Christ warned about Hell and taught His Disciples about Hell, which is why we are all to understand what the Bible teaches about Hell. Hell is a real place.

4. Another word, used nine times in referring to Hell in the New Testament, is the word, ***Abyss***, which is a special and specific place in Hades. It is 'the bottomless pit or place without bottom' and is specifically for fallen angels or demons. Remember each time the demons saw Christ coming near, they would cry out, *"Have you come to judge us before our time?"* and then begged Him to not cast them into the pit. Demons know that there is a day of judgment of

which they are scared. I wish sinners in our streets would cry out in that same manner. I wish they knew that there is a day of judgment coming. We are told about the *"beast that ascendeth"* out of the *"pit"* to make war with Israel in the last days (Rev.11:7; 17:8) and that the Dragon, otherwise known as the Old Serpent, the Devil or Satan, will be cast into the pit and imprisoned for a period of 1,000 years (Rev.20:1-3).

5. Another place mentioned which is either the same as the *Abyss* or at least similar, is **Tartarus** which means 'the deepest pit.' *"For if God spared not the angels that sinned, but cast them down to Hell* [Tartarus], *and delivered them into chains of darkness, to be reserved unto judgment..."* (II Pet.2:4). And again Jude speaks of such but without using this particular word but obviously speaking about the same thing: *"And the angels which kept not their first estate, but left their own habitation, he hath reserved in everlasting chains under darkness unto the judgment of the great day"* (1:6). Here angels are chained up in the deepest realms of Hell until judgment day because they sinned by not keeping their first estate. This speaks of a specific group of fallen angels but not of all those who fell with Lucifer. Those in *Tartarus* are held permanently until the judgment whereas the *Abyss* is a temporary holding place for wicked spirits.

6. Then there is the awful place, **Gehenna.** This is the NT Greek equivalent to the OT Hebrew *Tophet.* This was the place outside Jerusalem where the waste went. It was where the bodies of thieves and criminals were dumped and where a constantly smouldering fire burnt. It stank. It was a vile place where worms ate the flesh of men and animals amongst all the dung from that city. It was a putrid, vile place with a constant stench. *Gehenna* is used 12 times in the New Testament; 11 of which are by Christ. This is not a place which exists now but is a place which is to come. It is a place where the bodies and souls of sinners will be cast on that Day of Judgment. It is more than just Hell itself. Eight times it is mentioned in connection with the body going there; eight times it is mentioned in connection with fire;

eight times it is mentioned in the context of being everlasting.

7. The last and final place of punishment mentioned in the Bible is the **Lake of Fire**. After the Great White Throne judgment of all sinners we are told, *"And death and hell were cast into the lake of fire. This is the second death"* (Rev.20:14). Hades (Sheol) itself is cast into this final place of punishment as also is the beast, the false prophet, Satan and all those whose names are not written in the book of life (Rev.19:20; 20:10, 14-15; 21:8). Hades is not the final dwelling place of the wicked—the Lake of Fire is. While Christ is preparing mansions (dwelling places) in His house for the righteous, God is preparing the Lake of Fire and eternal punishment for Satan and for sinners.

THE RICH MAN AND LAZARUS

Christ taught the following. *"There was a certain rich man, which was clothed in purple and fine linen, and fared sumptuously every day: And there was a certain beggar named Lazarus, which was laid at his gate, full of sores, And desiring to be fed with the crumbs which fell from the rich man's table: moreover the dogs came and licked his sores. And it came to pass, that the beggar died, and was carried by the angels into Abraham's bosom: the rich man also died, and was buried; And in hell he lift up his eyes, being in torments, and seeth Abraham afar off, and Lazarus in his bosom. And he cried and said, Father Abraham, have mercy on me, and send Lazarus, that he may dip the tip of his finger in water, and cool my tongue; for I am tormented in this flame. But Abraham said, Son, remember that thou in thy lifetime receivedst thy good things, and likewise Lazarus evil things: but now he is comforted, and thou art tormented. And beside all this, between us and you there is a great gulf fixed: so that they which would pass from hence to you cannot; neither can they pass to us, that would come from thence. Then he said, I pray thee therefore, father, that thou wouldest send him to my father's house: For I have five brethren; that he may testify unto them, lest they also come into this place of torment. Abraham saith unto him, They have Moses and the* *prophets; let them hear them. And he said, Nay, father Abraham: but if one went unto them from the dead, they will repent. And he said unto him, If they hear not Moses and the prophets, neither will they be persuaded, though one rose from the dead"* (Luke 16:19-31).

The poor man Lazarus in his lifetime was poor and suffered much but when he died he was rewarded. On the contrary, the rich man had everything in his lifetime, but when he died he was tormented in Hell. From this story which Christ tells us we are told a few things about Hell:

1. We are told that in Hell men can see; men in Hell have eyes: *"And in hell he lift up his eyes...and seeth Abraham afar off, and Lazarus in his bosom"* (Lk.16:23). The rich man saw and recognised others.

2. We are told that in Hell men are tormented. It was in a state of *"...being in torments"* that he *"lifted up his eyes."* This word *"torments"*, *(basanos)*, is where we get our word 'base' or 'bottom' from. It literally means to get to the bottom of something or to have something revealed. It is used for a torture-chamber when a person is questioned and examined. It means to cause great pain through the means of torture. The means of this torture is fire.

3. We see that in Hell men pray. *"And he cried and said, Father Abraham, have mercy on me...for I am tormented in this flame."* Every sinner will become a praying man and woman. Every atheist is going to pray one day. They will be crying out, daily, for deliverance. Men can cry out now and have their prayer answered, but on the day that they enter Hell that opportunity comes to an end. No man in Hell will ever have his prayer for deliverance or mercy answered.

4. In Hell men Remember. *"...Abraham said, Son, remember that thou in thy lifetime receivedst thy good things, and likewise Lazarus evil things: but now he is comforted, and thou art tormented."* Men will remember houses, jobs, lands, family, friends...but they will not be able to enjoy one of these things. You may have thought

much of those things in this life, but in Hell the memories will torment man.

5. <u>In Hell men Thirst</u>. Hell is a place of eternal thirst without relief. *"...have mercy on me, and send Lazarus, that he may dip the tip of his finger in water, and cool my tongue; for I am tormented in this flame."* How much water could you carry to a man? If you dipped your finger in water, how much would that be? Yet the tormented man is asking for just a dip of the finger. Remember, this is what Christ taught saints!

6. <u>In Hell men care about their Family</u>. *"I pray thee therefore, father, that thou wouldest send him to my father's house: For I have five brethren; that he may testify unto them, lest they also come into this place of torment."* Men in Hell care about their brothers, their sisters, their mothers, their fathers, their children. Men in Hell would do anything to warn a man on the street to not dare go to Hell. A man in Hell would beg a man on the street not to go there. Why does the Church not have that urgency? Men in Hell have more urgency than any one of us sitting in church! When is the last time you cried about someone going to Hell? When is the last time you couldn't sleep at night for worrying about your loved ones going to Hell? When is the last time you were so disturbed you did not want to eat your food, because you knew that someone you love or know is on their way to Hell? Men in Hell do not want their loved ones to go there.

What Happened when Christ died?

i) His body was put in a sepulchre (Mk.15:45-46), with the prophetic promise that His body would not see corruption or decay (Acts 2:27). Christ spoke often of His physical resurrection on the third day.

ii) His Spirit went to the Lord (Lk.23:46) *"Father, into thy hands I commend <u>my spirit</u>:"*

iii) His soul went to Hades. *"...thou wilt not leave <u>my soul</u> in hell [hades], neither wilt thou suffer thine Holy One to see corruption"* (Acts 2:27). Hades had two sections.

We know this from reading of Lazarus who was rewarded and comforted with Abraham, Isaac, and Jacob, but the rich man who was tormented. The rich man looked over but could not cross over to them. Note: Abraham and all the other patriarchs could not go to Heaven yet as Christ had not yet died and risen, so they were there in Hades, in the inner bowels of the Earth, but on a higher plane than where the rich man was. *"...he also descended first into the lower parts of the earth"* (Eph.4:9). When Christ died he 'first' immediately descended into the lower parts of the Earth to Hades. Christ prophesied that He would go 'down' there: *"so shall the Son of man be three days and three nights in the heart of the earth"* (Mt.12:40). The Bible also tells us that Hades is *beneath* (Prov.15:24), *downward* (Eze.32:21) and in the *nether parts of the earth* (32:18).

So from this we can see that all men in the Old Testament, the righteous and the wicked, went down to Hades. Every single one of them descended into Hades, but on that third day when Christ rose from the dead, saints rose up from the dead with Him and walked the streets of Jerusalem. All the saints from all the ages rose up and ascended to Heaven. Paradise moved from Hades to Heaven. Remember, Christ promised the dying thief on the cross that, *"Today shalt thou be with me in paradise"* (Lk.23:43). Paradise is also called, *Abraham's bosom* (Lk.16:22); before the resurrection of Christ, Paradise was in Hades, the place of the dead. The thief went immediately to a place of comfort and blessing, where there was no suffering. Note: there is presently no limbo; there is no purgatory; there is no 'in-between' state.

In summary: In the Old Testament there was a place of comfort, reward, and 'waiting' called, Paradise which was in Hades, but it was moved to Heaven upon the resurrection of Christ.

Paul, in II Corinthians 12, talks about a man (himself) being caught up to the Third Heaven which is God's Heaven and Paul says that he was caught up into Paradise. *"...caught up to the third heaven [v2]...caught up into paradise [v4]"* So from this we see that after Christ's resurrection, Paradise is in the Third Heaven which is God's Throne. The Earth is the first Heaven, the second Heaven is the Universe, and the Third Heaven is God's Heaven where His throne is. Paradise that was once in the bowels of the Earth is now in the third Heaven.

GREAT WHITE THRONE JUDGMENT

The Great White Throne Judgment comes at the end of the Millennium which is the 1,000 year, physical reign of Christ upon the Earth. We believers stand at the judgment seat of Christ 1,000 years before this. We will have already been judged as to how we have lived, how we thought, how we acted, and then for 1,000 years we will reign upon the Earth with Jesus Christ.

Rev.20:4 *"And I saw thrones, and they* [the saints] *sat upon them, and judgment was given unto them: and I saw the souls of them that were beheaded for the witness of Jesus, and for the word of God, and which had not worshipped the beast, neither his image, neither had received his mark upon their foreheads, or in their hands; and they lived and reigned with Christ a thousand years."* The saints possess the kingdom. They are manifested as the people of God, just as Christ was manifest at His resurrection. One day we are going to be manifest. That body you are sitting in is not what it is all going to be about. There is a day when you will get raised again in a new incorruptible body. You will shine forth as the stars of Heaven after your judgment.

Rev.20:5 *"But the rest of the dead lived not again until the thousand years were finished. This is the first resurrection. Blessed and holy is he that hath part in the first resurrection: on such the second death hath no power, but they shall be priests of God and of Christ, and shall reign with him a thousand years. And when the thousand years are expired, Satan shall be loosed out of his prison..."*

Saints, the Righteous, who were judged at the judgment seat of Christ, will reign with Christ for 1,000 years after the 'First resurrection', but the remaining dead, the unsaved, who have never been resurrected, will remain in Hell, in torment, awaiting judgment for those one thousand years. They will not live again

144

until the thousand years have finished when they will then be resurrected in the 'Second resurrection' and this resurrection will be unto damnation. They will not receive their new resurrection body until this day at the end of the thousand years.

Rev.20:11-13, *"And I saw a great white throne, and him*[Christ] *that sat on it, from whose face the earth and the heaven fled away; and there was found no place for them. And I saw the dead,* [note this is the SECOND resurrection] *small and great* [those who had not been raised yet], *stand before God; and the books were opened: and another book was opened, which is the book of life: and the dead were judged out of those things which were written in the books, according to their works. And the sea gave up the dead which were in it; and death and hell delivered up the dead which were in them: and they were judged every man according to their works."* The Second Resurrection is the physical resurrection of every man and woman in Hell. When a man dies there is a delay in that judgment. He is awaiting his judgment which will be pronounced on that day. *"The Lord knoweth how to...reserve the unjust unto the day of judgment to be punished"* (II Pet.2:9). God is keeping them for that day. All those who died in their sins are presently in Hell and are suffering now but they will be resurrected with a new body to face the judgment. We know this because Christ speaks of not only casting the soul into *Gehenna* but the body as well (Mt.5:29-30; Mt.10:28).

Every man and every woman is going to stand before Him and the books will be opened; books with records of every aspect of their lives. Hitler is going to stand there. Judas is going to stand there. Lot's wife will be there. Herod is going to stand there. Someone's granny is going to be there on that judgment day. It is a, 'GREAT THRONE' because everything is put right. It is a WHITE throne because it speaks of His holiness, His purity, and His righteousness. There is no pride at that Throne. There is nobody laughing and scorning. Christ will sit upon that Throne and judge every man for his rejection of the Gospel. He will judge a man for rejecting that tract he was handed one Saturday morning in Limerick. He will judge men for rejecting the sister or the brother who was pleading with them to believe on Christ. All that will be brought before them and God will be seen as the absolute righteous judge. This is everlasting judgment.

Rev.20:14 *"And death and hell were cast into the lake of fire. This is the second death."* At this great judgment of sinners at the end of the Millennium God is also going to destroy the Heavens and the Earth. *"But the heavens and the earth, which are now, by the same word are kept in store, reserved unto fire against the day of judgment and perdition of ungodly men"* (II Pet.3:7). So the Earth is also reserved until the time of this judgment and unto destruction by fire just as sinners are reserved until the judgment and then cast in the lake of fire. When it says in this verse that the "Heavens" are reserved unto fire it does not mean God's Heaven but the second Heaven, the atmospheric Heavens.

The Bible tells us that God is going to cast Hell into the *"lake of fire"* (Rev.19:20; 20:10, 14-15). Hell and the Lake of Fire are not the same. Hell is going to be cast INTO the Lake of Fire. Then God will cast all the unbelievers into that Lake of Fire. All hypocrites, all atheists will be thrown into the Lake of Fire. Death itself will be thrown into the Lake of Fire. Death is the last enemy and it will be cast into Hell. Then God will wrap everything up and make a new Heaven and a new Earth.

Matthew 25 speaks of *"Everlasting [aionios] punishment"* (Mt.25:46) that word *everlasting* is everlasting! Hell is everlasting. There is a popular teaching today that says that Hell is not everlasting. It teaches that you go somewhere for a short time but then you get burnt up and destroyed. This teaching is called Annihilationism. But Hell is most surely EVERLASTING.

This word *everlasting (ainios)* is referred to 69 times in the New Testament:

- 7 times regarding Heaven,
- 6 times regarding The Gospel,
- 3 times regarding God,
- 2 times regarding Eternity before creation,
- 44 times regarding Eternal life,
- 7 times regarding the punishment of the wicked.

If we make Hell to be only a short time then we make *everlasting life* to be only a short time because what God says about eternal life, He says about eternal punishment. If we change the meaning of this word in reference to eternal punishment or eternal judgment, as many modern teachers do, then we will unravel every other doctrinal truth where this word is used.

We are also told in Revelation 14:11 concerning the punishment of the wicked: *"And the smoke of their torment ascendeth up for ever and ever: and they have no rest day nor night."* Again many of these teachers dispute that *"for ever and ever"* actually does not mean forever. But again if we simply test this with the Word of God we find out how erroneous this statement is.

This term *"for ever and ever"* is found 14 times in the Book of Revelation:

- 6 times regarding the Father,
- 4 times regarding the Son,
- 3 times regarding endless punishment,
- 1 time regarding the reign of the saints.

We read of Paul standing trial before Felix, the Roman Governor of Judea: *"And as he reasoned of righteousness, temperance, and judgment to come, Felix trembled, and answered, Go thy way for this time; when I have a convenient season, I will call for thee"* (Acts 24:25). As a local leader, Felix, a man with power, calls Paul out to judgment. Paul is in chains yet Paul reasons with Felix and reminds him of the day when he will stand in judgment before God. Paul warns Felix that he will be accountable for every action. He tells Felix that he will be responsible for the Gospel that Paul preached to him. We are told that Felix began to 'tremble' because Paul was preaching concerning a coming judgment.[10]

---

[10] Marcus Antonius Felix was Governor of Judea from about 52-59 AD. It is obvious from the text that he was fascinated by Paul's message and impressed by Paul, but he was controlled by a desire for bribes. Because of trouble caused by his negligence he was ordered back to Rome to stand trial but escaped condemnation because of his brothers influence at court. It would seem that he continued to live a sinful life but we have no record of his last days. The testimony however is left here that he trembled under the message of coming

147

Saints, we believers ARE MEANT TO PREACH ABOUT COMING JUDGMENT! Paul preached it. It is New Covenant. It is an act of the Grace of God that you can stand before sinners and warn them that there is a day of judgment. Most men and women know this but they close their ears and their conscience to it. There is a day coming when there will no longer be mercy; there will no longer be forgiveness. On that day as we look around we will be embarrassed that we did so little to warn men. There will be tears from saints who did not do all they could in warning others but Revelation 21:4 says, *"And God shall wipe away all tears from their eyes..."* There will be tears in the life to come, but only momentarily.

Friends, as we close this message on the sixth and final *foundational truth* mentioned in Hebrews chapter 6, we close on a sober and serious note. If this truth was taught and laid into each and every Christian life at the beginning of their walk with God then I am certain their life would be lived differently. They would be gripped with a view of Eternity and would live their life in great earnest. May the Lord help us now to weep over men on their way to Hell and make us rejoice in the hope of future reward, comfort, and blessing.

---

judgment and we can be sure that he will not escape that coming judgment.

CHAPTER 8

GOING ON TO PERFECTION

I believe that this truth of 'Going on to Perfection' can be considered one of the most neglected, disbelieved, mocked, downgraded, and embarrassing of truths amongst professing believers today. It is a lost jewel, a precious truth, a vital need, an urgent requirement and a heavenly joy.

But before we come to this last lesson on Christian Foundations, allow me to reiterate how important these foundations are. The foundation of your house is the most important part of your house or any building, but how much more so are these spiritual foundations to your walk with God. This is no light subject for if the foundation is wrong everything is wrong.

It says in **Psalm 11:3,** *"If the foundations be destroyed, what can the righteous do?"* In our society or in our church, if the very foundation of God is destroyed, what can even a righteous man do? It is very hard to operate or move in the things of God if the very foundation is destroyed. Therefore, it is vital that we give ourselves to study this issue of foundations. If we mess up the foundations, forget the building. If you are looking to minster or do something for the Lord, you must look at these foundations.

Hebrews 2:10, *"For it became him, for whom are all things, and by whom are all things, in bringing many sons unto glory, to make the captain* [Jesus] *of their salvation perfect through sufferings."*

Hebrews 5:9-6:3, *"And being made perfect, he* [Jesus] *became the author of eternal salvation unto all them that obey him; Called of God an high priest after the order of Melchisedec. Of whom we have many things to say, and hard to be uttered, seeing ye are dull of hearing. For when for the time ye ought to be teachers, ye have need that one teach you again which be the* *first principles of the oracles of God; and are become such as have need of milk, and not of strong meat. For every one that useth milk is unskilful in the word of righteousness: for he is a babe. But strong meat belongeth to them that are of full age, even those who by reason of use have their senses exercised to discern both good and evil. Therefore leaving the principles of the doctrine of Christ, let us go on unto perfection; not laying again the foundation of repentance from dead works, and of faith toward God, Of the doctrine of baptisms, and of laying on of hands, and of resurrection of the dead, and of eternal judgment. And this will we do, if God permit."*

The goal of what we are doing or the goal of these teachings is not to stay with these foundations. The goal is something beyond these foundations. The goal is something far more than these foundations for we are called to go on to perfection.

In the book of Hebrews, we read the word 'Heaven(s)' 17 times, because Hebrews is a book not about Earth but about heavenly, spiritual things; things not of this world. Also, we read the word 'eternal' 15 times and this is not accidental. The Holy Spirit is making this emphasis because He wants to draw out our hearts; to be conscience of something. He wants to draw our eyes away from the temporal or away from time and set them upon Eternity. He wants to draw our attention away from the things of this world unto Eternal things.

We must not be ignorant of the working of the Holy Spirit. Many times the Holy Spirit will come to our gathering and will look to draw our attention. He is looking to warn you about something that is around the corner and if we trust Him, He will speak in our meetings. The Holy Spirit will warn, encourage and equip you for what you are going through and for what you will go through. If we sit in dullness, not alert we will miss something vital to our walk with God.

Furthermore, the words '**perfect, perfection and perfected** are used <u>14 times</u> in this epistle. Again, the Holy Spirit is trying to emphasize this and if you miss this, then you have missed the point of the book of Hebrews. In a nutshell, the book of Hebrews is about the heavenly life; about eternal life not bound by time; it is about a state of perfection which is not restricted to babyhood or childishness; it is a call to go on to complete maturity and utter perfection.

Concerning *'going on top perfection'*, we see Paul saying that he wants to speak to the Hebrews about CHRIST: *"Of whom we have many things to say, and hard to be uttered, seeing ye are dull of hearing"* (Heb.5:11). Paul wants to tell them of the fullness and breadth of Christ, not just about doctrines, not just about theology, but concerning the person of Christ in all His glory. Paul wants them to experience, to know and to understand the fullness and depths of Christ. But he says that there are some things hard to explain or to layout clearly. This is why we must come to the Word of God prayerfully and in faith. We cannot just understand it academically. We must come with a heart hungry for Christ. **If you want to learn the Bible, learn it on your knees.**

I failed every exam at school, apart from an 'A' in Art. I was not academic and could barely put my 'Bs' and 'Ds' the correct way around, but I have learnt the Bible on my knees. In prayer and fasting I would cry out to God, "Speak to me, Lord, speak to me, teach me, minister to me. I do not want just knowledge. I am coming to this book to have my heart enlarged that I might know Christ and that I might experience something of His vital reality." That was what my heart hungered for—not intellectual knowledge. Knowledge puffs up but when you get filled with a revelation of God's Word you will be edified and will edify one another and that is true spiritual knowledge, but if it is mere head knowledge you will get puffed up. Someone who is puffed up will merely want to impart information and dead knowledge—that is barren and of no spiritual consequence whatsoever. But a humble sincere believer will want to take others into deeper places in Christ Jesus. When you know the things of God you will desire to see others come into it in true reality. That is spirituality.

Heb.5:11, *"Of whom we have many things to say, and hard to be uttered, seeing ye are dull of hearing."* It is hard to explain, or hard to make clear to them, first of all because they think that they know all there is to know about Christ! Paul wants to take them into the depths, fullness, and breadths of revelation concerning Christ—not only of His earthly ministry but of His heavenly ministry as our Intercessor and High Priest. Paul is saying that it is not sufficient to just know that He died on the Cross for your sins and rose again on the third day, (thank God you do know that) but he is saying that there is a breadth and depth of Christ's ministry now, 'within the veil', spiritually, in Heaven to which Paul wants their eyes to be opened because it will encourage them and establish them. **Seeing Christ's heavenly ministry will make us to walk with God.**

BUT Paul says that he cannot explain to them or take the Hebrews into these truths because they are *'dull of hearing'.* Paul wants to speak concerning Christ in His High Priestly ministry but **is hindered by the spiritual state of the hearers.**

In verse 12, it says that they *"are **become** such as have **need** of milk."* Paul uses the word **'become'** because they were not always like this; they were at a different place at some point previously. They had been taught the things of God. They had a great breadth and understanding about Christ. They were once able to eat the meat of the Word, but what they once had they no longer have. Through their dullness of hearing their spiritual maturity was lost or blemished. This can happen to anyone of us. Without growth in the spiritual life even knowledge is lost or at least it becomes dead. It makes no difference if you have been saved 50 years, 10 years or one year, there is a state of dullness that can come to you. It was not there at the beginning of your salvation. You could have walked ten years with Christ and may have great testimonies, experiences, and all sorts of knowledge, but if dullness ever comes in, it will have a spiritual effect upon you. Paul says here concerning these consequences that the Hebrews had become 'such as need milk'. They had lost something in their spiritual walk. They had old testimonies, experiences, knowledge, and respect from others and even years of experience (although not spiritual maturity) yet they have **"become"** as **"babes."**

He is saying, "You may be born-again and still love Jesus; you may still believe all the same things, but you have lost something you used to have. There is a knowledge that you used to have; a vitality you used to have; a walk with God that you no longer have, through *dullness of hearing."* **We must be very conscious that spiritual maturity can be lost**—we are not talking about salvation here—but your spiritual maturity can be blemished and you may need to go back to baby food or milk.

Can you imagine if a grown man who had once lived as a mature man had to return back to infantile actions, to being bottle fed and needing his nappy (diaper) changed for him? This would not be a happy state of affairs! Everyone would know that something tragic had happened and yet I have observed this down over the years, time after time, where someone who had great experiences or knowledge, literally went back to a baby stage in their spirituality due to the present condition of their heart. They retained their knowledge and could still give you many facts. They could still tell you about experiences that they had yet they lost the place of maturity and spirituality through dullness of hearing.

Are you hearing me? You can spend years walking with God but lose your maturity.

You can lack intellect but if you have a true spiritual heart, you will have a true understanding of the things of God that an academically intellectual person will never understand. The Bible says that the Father has hidden these things from such persons. *"Jesus answered and said, I thank thee, O Father, Lord of heaven and earth, because thou hast hid these things from the wise and prudent, and hast revealed them unto babes"* (Mt.11:25). If we just have a right heart toward Him, He will open up the windows of Heaven and the depths of the revelation of His Word.

Of what worth are old testimonies if you do not live in a vital experience with God? They are a hollow sounding cymbal. You can talk about things that happened—they are true—but if it is not real and vital in the present, it is a dead, clanging cymbal. If you lose the reality of walking with Christ, your knowledge, your experience, your testimony is nothing. All we need to have is a simple day by day walk with Jesus Christ.

Back in the Old Testament, they had to go out and gather that manna, which is a type of the Word of God, and if they tried to keep too much for the next day, it rotted, worms ate it, and it was of no value to them. Daily they had to go out and collect just enough fresh manna to feed themselves.

Note: Paul is writing to the Hebrew churches which were born in revival. Some of the believers he is writing to would have had over thirty or forty years of experience as Christians. But this does not mean that these years were used effectually in walking with God. They could have told you firsthand accounts of Peter's ministry, of outpourings of the Spirit and genuine revivals, of miracles and healings, yet they had regressed to being babies.

Saints, it is not about walking with God for a certain number of years. It is not about knocking up enough hours of meetings that makes you spiritually mature. You can be fifty years walking as a Christian but still be a babe! **The state of maturity has nothing to do with years; it has everything to do with a depth of fellowship with Christ and the ability to hear what He is saying.**

Another Apostle Echoes These Warnings

John, in writing the book of Revelation, records Christ's words to the church at Sardis, in Asia, *"I* [Christ] *know thy works, that thou hast a name that thou livest, and art dead"* (**Rev.3:1**). In other words the church at Sardis had a reputation—an outward appearance of life—but no true spiritual maturity. If you walked into a meeting of the Sardis church you would think, "These people are alive! This church has a great testimony!" They might even be able to tell you testimonies which would amaze you, but when Christ looked at their hearts and peeled back the cover of their spiritual state, He said, "You have a reputation that you are alive but you are actually dead!" That was Christ's observation. **All the outward show of religion does not mean a nickel! If Christ does not think you are spiritual or spiritually mature then the outward appearance means nothing.**

Again John records Christ's words, to the church at Philadelphia: *"Behold, I come quickly: hold that fast which thou hast, that no man take thy crown"* (**Rev.3:11**). In other words, someone CAN TAKE YOUR CROWN. Here are good believers who do have a crown because they have been running well, fighting the fight, walking with God, but they are warned that if they are not careful, someone will steal their crown.

I have walked with believers over the years that have had all the visions, all the charisma, all the gifts, or all the eloquence but I watched them: they were not faithful, they were not careful and when they dropped their crown, I said, "Lord, I will take it. If they are not going to be faithful, I will be faithful." If you do not obey God, He will raise someone else up to do what He asked you to do. If you want to stay as a babe, you will get to Heaven, but God will use somebody else. You need to *hold fast* if you want to be useful to God.

Some in the ministry struggle and fight with their own inabilities because they feel that others more gifted should be doing it. The truth is however, that those with such gifting have lost the spiritual maturity to enable them to minister effectually for God. They were not willing to pay the price. They were not willing to grow. We may lack in many things but we are to be faithful unto God, fight the Devil, and go through. Lack of ability never scared me as much as not being faithful to what God has called me to. I have seen people who were given everything as far as gifting and calling, yet they were not faithful. They will get to Heaven but they will have no reward because they did not fulfil the will of God.

Their spiritual hearing has become *"dull"* which is the Greek word, *nothros,* meaning sluggish, lazy, stupid (not intellectually stupid but 'stupid' in not desiring or understanding the things of God). This is not talking about those in this world who have a 'simple mind' (God will not judge the 'feebleminded') but this is talking about a lazy person, a sluggish Christian who is lazy about spiritual things. They are dull of hearing or in other words Paul is saying, "I cannot speak to them. I cannot get through to them. Though I am knocking, you cannot hear because of your spiritual condition." **Being lazy is a deliberate thing. It is not accidental to be lazy.** Being lazy is not a case of not understanding or grasping these things. It is a laziness of heart toward God. If you are lazy towards man you may get off with it, but if you are lazy in this walk with God, it will catch up with you.

The word, *nothros,* is taken from, *nothos,* which means *'an illegitimate son'* and the same word is translated *"slothful"* in Hebrews 6:12. It is used there as a warning that you, *"be not slothful, but followers of them who through faith and patience inherit the promises."* In other words, to be sluggish or lazy in your heart, is to act as if you are not God's son. No child of a king should act like this. No child of the living God, of Christ, should act like this. You should not be lazy over spiritual things. God has opened up His treasures and shown you that Heaven and Earth is going to pass away and that those that do the will of God will remain and abide forever. Nothing will hinder them. Those that do the will of God will outlast this old planet. If you obey the Word of God you will still be 'here' when your own country no longer exists. When time is no more, they who abide in the Lord will continue into Eternity.

Note that in the warning in Hebrews 6:12, Paul gives us the opposite of being slothful, *"but followers of them who through faith and patience inherit the promises."* So the opposite of being slothful is to watch with patience, diligence, and faith. Do you come to the Word of God with faith in your heart? Do you go to the prayer meeting determined to break through? Do you determine to rise above discouragement or do you sit about feeling sorry for yourself? Will you sit there 'til you die? Rise up and fight some demon; fight through some discouragement; fight through some mental argument. All of us have those battles. Thoughts build up in the mind and can start to weigh us down but this is when we should rise up with faith and begin to fight and the weight and discouragements will break!

There is a distinction between **healthy babes** in Christ and **carnal babes**. There is a time when it is right to be a babe. There is a time when it is 'ok' to be a child. There is a time when it is 'ok' to be immature, to play in the streets, and play games but when you are older, some things need to change. Toys need to be put away and some things need to go in the bin. But there is an unnatural stage which the Bible refers to as 'carnal babes' which refers to those who are stuck at the baby stage which is not a healthy stage. A 'carnal babe' is fleshly, and worldly. They are in the wrong place at the wrong time, doing the wrong thing. You can always tell you are not moving on spiritually because the scenery never changes. In the same way spiritually, if nothing ever changes and you are going in circles for years, then you are stuck at a baby stage. Decades can pass and some people grumble and complain about the same things year in and year out. These are people who are stuck at baby stage; a carnal baby stage. They say, "If only something will change...", when all the time it is them who need to change. This is completely different to someone who is newly born-again, who loves Christ but may not know much. This healthy baby has not yet attained unto a walk with God in fullness and in its depths. This healthy baby is not sanctified in all areas but he does want to be.

For example, brother B.H. Clendennen struggled with smoking for around 18 months after his conversion. At the time, many people put him in Hell for that. Many people would have put him out of the church and doubted his salvation because he was still struggling with it, but he hated it. He wanted to be free of it and a day did come when he was totally set free and never wanted to go back to it. We do not excuse such things as smoking, neither do we make light of them or say that they are 'ok', but with spiritual growth the believer will grow out of them.

Dirtying your nappy at a baby stage is expected, but somewhere down the road, we will expect you to grow out of dirtying your nappy or spilling your food all over the table. If such growth does not take place then we will need to sit down and talk about it. We must not ignore it. There is a difference between being stuck at a baby stage and being a baby because you are new-born.

The Hebrews had returned to and settled back at this carnal baby stage. This whole book of Hebrews is written to stir up these believers to rise up out of their stunted growth and to press on to perfection in Christ Jesus. No true minister will ever accept immaturity, carnality, or worldliness as normal or healthy in the church. Let us take heed to this and note:

THE MARKS OF *"CARNAL BABES"*

i)   Carnal babes are marked by immaturity, foolishness, and childishness. A child acts like a child: foolish and silly. There is a great immaturity in a child. In a spiritual babe everything is light, everything is foolish. On the other hand you can meet a 15 year old and see that there is a great maturity in them. Now this is not saying that this maturity is a result of an intellectual ability, but rather it is something of character: they have matured quickly; they are serious; everything is not a joke to them; they have forsaken lightness.

ii) Carnal babes are carnal; they are natural. By the word 'carnal' in the New Testament, Paul means that they are carnal or sensual: they live by their five senses. Everything is natural: they have not learnt to walk by the Spirit. They are not living with the reality of Heaven above them; instead they are moved by their emotions and circumstances which dominate their life. That is carnality. It does not mean you are out sinning, it just means you have not learnt to live beyond the natural feelings and emotions.

iii) Carnal babes are not able to apply the Word of God to their own lives: They do not live up to the Word of God. They are not an example or a testimony. You will never take anyone anywhere where you have not been yourself. If you do not apply the Word to yourself, do not try to tell anyone else how to live. If you have an area out of order in your own life, you have no right to tell someone else how to do it. That is back-to-front. Show me someone who is truly walking in the truth of God's Word: they can come and tell me authoritatively what to do because they are an example of it. I would only ask a qualified mechanic to help me with a problem in my car because he knows what he is doing! I am absolutely persuaded that a qualified mechanic is not pretending; he is not a hypocrite; he understands the engine. Just because someone has a badge, oil on their face and dirt on their hands does not mean that they are a mechanic. A pretender will not produce the goods. A real mechanic only has to listen to the engine and will most likely know what the problem is. I am only going to allow that mechanic that knows what he is doing to work on my car, not the pretender.

A carnal babe may have 'been a Christian for many years' and have had years of experience but if they are not living in a *vital reality* of fellowship with Christ and walking in obedience to the Word they are carnal. Saints, whether you are saved a few weeks or a few months, if someone comes to you and has all the testimonies of years past, please know that it means nothing unless they are walking with Christ. Look for those who walk with Christ and follow their example. Do not listen to those who only have stories to tell you! Look for people who are walking with Christ now. Avoid those who only want to lead you into an experience of head knowledge or some manifestation of the 'spirit'. Someone who is truly walking with Christ will not just try to *push* you in that direction, but will rather say, "Follow me, because I am following Christ! If I am not following Christ, do not follow my example. Test my life with the Word of God."

iv) Carnal babes always excuse their immaturity: Carnal babes cover over their immaturity with spiritual language. They are all talk but very little walk. Such babes ought to be deeply broken by the Word of God that speaks into their spiritual condition and which challenges them to grow up. Those who excuse their spiritually immature condition are actually exalting their opinions and excuses above the commands of Scripture.

v) Carnal babes never take responsibility: Carnal babes never take responsibility for their own spiritual condition. It is always someone else or something else which takes the blame for their immaturity. To take full responsibility for your condition, words, or actions is maturity.

vi) Carnal babes always want to lighten the intensity of God's Word, obscure its clarity, and lower its standard: The Word of God shows up a carnal babe for what they are. They attempt to lower the Gospel or lighten the Word of God so that they 'fit it' or look good or better. That is a very dangerous spiritual place to be! Do not mess with God's Word. There are many sinners who love their sin and acknowledge their guilt but they do not change the Word of God to justify themselves. Sadly, though, there are many spiritual babes amongst God's people who endeavour to change the Word to justify their spiritual condition. That is extremely dangerous ground to stand on. It is far better and healthier to say, "I have sinned. I have fallen short. I am guilty," than to play and tamper with the Word! Carnal babes try to de-spiritualize the commands of God. They say: "That's extreme" or "That's only for the first century" or "That is not for me or you. We cannot live up to everything written in the Bible." Saints, if we change the Word of God that easily we may as well throw it out. The Word of God is the gauge; the marker; the eternal unchanging standard.

In both Ezekiel and Revelation, the angel of the Lord has a ruler and begins to measure everything in the house of God. By this, God is saying that everything has to be according to God's pattern. We must not lower the Word to accommodate to the world, your opinion, or your lifestyle. No, no, no! We are commanded to go on toward perfection. Never bring the Word of God down to an earthly realm. Rather, let us stir our hearts to say that we want to go on to heavenly places. I do not want to stay an earthbound, carnal, immature Christian. I want to really walk with God and go somewhere with Him.

In verse 12, Paul speaking to 'mature' (in years) Christians says, *"...ye have **need** that one teach you again which be the first principles..."* That word *"need"* means, **it is now necessary** that much effort go towards getting them back to a spiritual position. He is saying to them that they will not go anywhere in their walk unless they come back to these basic principles again. They need to get established in the milk of the Word once again. How humiliating for these 'mature' (in years) believers to have to go back to milk. **Please note Saints, you can lose spiritual maturity!** You can lose years of walking with God! You can lose the ability to eat meat! That ought to be a warning to us. Do not be sluggish! Do not be slow of heart! Do not take meetings casually! Everything that happens in the house of God is for your edification so that you can go through with God. If you consciously decide to not be in a meeting, then that is a reflection of the state of your heart. (Of course we understand that there are genuine reasons for not being in a meeting. We would not at all want to put any unnecessary burden on anyone. But let us be alert to this.)

In verse 13, he says, *"For every one that useth milk is **unskilful in the word** of righteousness:"* That word *unskilful* means to be inexperienced, to have no-experience; to be ignorant or lacking in skill or ability. The *word of righteousness* is the meat; the deep things of God. The *word of righteousness* is for the mature or those who really walk with God. The man who finds himself unable to eat meat and who can only feed on milk has lost his maturity. This man can claim many things but they are not a reality. The *ability* which Paul refers to here is the *ability* to apply the Word of God to one's own life.

The *'strong meat'* which is the word of righteousness is only for those who are of *full age*. The person of full age is truly spiritually mature. Paul is presenting two ends of the spectrum to us: on one end the spiritual babe who is at the beginning of his walk and on the other those who spiritually are fully mature saints. These are two very different vital healthy stages in the believer's life.

Notice too that **inconsistency marks babes.** Paul calls the Corinthians *"carnal"* (sensual) and *"babes"* in his first letter to them (I Cor.3:1, 3, 4) and rebukes them for tolerating *"fornication"* (I Cor.5:1). But in his second letter he has to write and tell them to forgive the same person (2:7). **Babes are marked by extremism.** One moment they ignore sin the next they are too hard on it. There is no balance or real ability to discern. This is inconsistency and it is the mark of a babe (carnal Christians).

How do we grow or make this journey to maturity?

In verse 14, Paul tells us how to get off the milk, step by step, and how to go on to maturity: *"those who by reason of use have their senses exercised to discern both good and evil."*

i)   *"by reason of use"*: the word *use* here means a habit, a practise or a custom. He is talking about something that is in constant and continual use. These are people who have made diligent use of the Word. They have searched the breadths, depths, and fullness of Christ. I would hate to think that I could pass through decades of Christian life and yet be ignorant of much of the knowledge of the depths of Christ. After twenty years, I should not be only talking about, 'He died for me and showed me grace'—you know very well that we do not take that lightly at all because such things are fundamental, foundational and central—but the fact is Christ saved you to walk with Him. Christ did not save you just to get you out of Hell and into Heaven. This Christian life is not just 'fire insurance'. He saved you so that you could move into a place of maturity that He might have someone with whom He can commune, walk with, and to whom He could reveal Himself. You and I were not born to stay as babes! You and I are born to go on into mature spirituality and into the depths of Christ and the way to make this journey is *by reason of use,* **by habitually exercising your senses.**

ii)   *"senses exercised."* Babies have all their five *"senses"* when they are born but they lack the ability and experience in using them. They do not know how to accurately use the information which their senses feed to their brain. After about six months, an infant will know how to use that mouth! A baby is made to make noise which soon becomes speech. The day you were born-again, God gave you spiritual senses. He opened your eyes, your ears and gave you a new heart which began to feel things that you had never felt before (some believers down through the ages have even smelled the 'fragrance of Christ'). God gave you spiritual faculties when you were born-again which you did not have when you were dead in your sins. Paul is saying that by using these faculties, you will grow. That baby gets into every cupboard, it goes up and down the stairs backwards, and whatever way they can because there is a life in them and they learn very quickly. Paul is saying that the believer needs to exercise their ability to see, ability to hear, ability to feel and ability to walk with God otherwise the believer will be stunted in their growth. The word *"exercised"* here is the Greek word, *gumnazo* where we get our word for gymnasium or gym which was the word used in the Greek language for those who practised or trained for athletic games. So he is saying here that believers are to habitually and constantly exercise those senses to become mature in Christ. He is not asking you to do something miraculous, he is just asking you to use what God has given to you at your new birth. You did not open your own blind eyes. You did not change your own heart. He gave you the ability to discern the presence of God. Who is it that tells you when God is in a meeting? Who tells you that He is there meeting with you around the Lord's Table? You cannot see Him with your natural eyes but it is HE who gives you the senses to gaze on Him spiritually. We can catch a sight of Him as we meet together in prayer or in the midst of worship. We CAN feel God's presence and that is a faculty to be exercised. Two people can be in a meeting and one feels the presence of God but the other does not. Two people can be in a meeting and one hears God but one does not. One can have a burning heart whilst the other sitting beside him is as dead as a doornail.

iii) *"to discern both good and evil."* Those who grow by exercising these God-given faculties can **discern** between the good (valuable) and the evil (worthless). This word *"discern"* (*diakrisis*) means to separate thoroughly; to discriminate; to weigh or judge between that which is valuable and that which is worthless. They can discern between that which is valuable and that which is worthless in their own life. That is a place of maturity. You can look at your own life and separate or segregate between that which is of eternal worth, which is rewarded on the Day of Judgment, and that which is pointless or carnal. It may not be overt sin, but you discern that which is of no consequence and that which is of great consequence. A child does not see that they are walking into a situation that will burn them. A baby does not understand to not touch the hot plate which will burn them. They need to be told and even still will often touch it anyway. That experience will teach them. One can tell a Christian, "Don't do it!" yet 50% will immediately go ahead and do it. New Christians often take a word of wisdom as a mere 'opinion' when it can actually be coming out of years of study, years of watching the same scenarios happen over and over again and years of a walk with God. Young believer, know this: a word of wisdom will help you grow in Jesus Christ.

When I was a wee boy, I watched my two big brothers get punished for being naughty or rather for disobeying my parents. I watched them stand outside my dad's door with tears running down their cheeks (they could almost feel the pain before they received it!) waiting on our Dad for the consequence of their wrong-doing. Now I failed most things at school, but I could do arithmetic and in my little mind I added up and equated the situation: 'if you disobey and do wrong you will find yourself standing at Dad's door and will receive a punishment.' So I decided and willed that I would not be naughty or do something wrong. I learnt a great deal from their pain. Because I studied this, I worked out that I did not need to go through that myself. But in the church, we too often see people making the same mistakes over, and over, and over again without learning anything.

Over the years, I tried to warn leaders and churches in Ireland not to go the way that churches have in Britain. I warned them not to go with the gimmicks and games which have led to dire consequences in many other nations. Sadly though, I have watched as leaders led their churches into the same spiritual cul-de-sacs and then watched them suffer the very same consequences. I warned them how much the youth have been ruined by these games of religion, yet church by church I have watched them fall. They keep going on the same road because it is popular and contemporary.

Heb.6:1, *"Therefore leaving the principles of the doctrine of Christ, let us go on unto perfection."* Paul is encouraging them and us to move beyond the foundation which is solid. He is not saying that we should ignore or leave behind the foundation but rather that on the basis of this foundation we go on and build toward perfection. He does not mean that we leave repentance or that we have moved on from repentance never to repent again, rather he reiterates that such foundations are the only foundation and that is what you build on. In fact he emphasises in these verses that if there is any loss of this foundation in our lives then we must come back and repair them before moving forward once more. If you remove the foundation there will be no building.

Please note: the baptism in the Holy Ghost is in this foundation. It is not just for the mature. The baptism in the Holy Ghost is not a deep teaching, it is a simple teaching. We can think that the baptism in the Holy Ghost is a great place of depth and maturity, when it is elementary. The baptism will get you out of that place of babyhood and immaturity but it is elementary; it is part of the 'ABC's. Do not just stay at the baptism of the Holy Ghost. Move on to maturity in Christ.

Whole churches and movements build around faith, or water baptism, or the baptism in the Holy Ghost, or some gift, or some special doctrine whereas we are called to press on to a full experience of Jesus Christ.

In verse 1, he says, *"not laying again the foundation"*. The word *again* means not laying the foundations anew or once more or repeating the process. Our churches should change; they should not stay the same year in and year out. If someone visits your fellowship after being away for 10 years, they should not be saying, "Hallelujah, you are just like you used to be!" No—they should see a change; they should see that the church has moved on. They ought to note maturity; that you are speaking of the depths in Christ of which you did not speak before. They ought to recognize that the fellowship has moved on. This does not mean that we change things for the sake of changing—we are not going to change the worship style just for the sake of changing. This does not mean that we become user-friendly and forgo standards like wearing a tie. This does not mean that the preachers stop getting excited, preach more quietly, or calm down. Those who think that such actions are a sign of spiritual maturity are foolish. The visitor should note rather that individually, and as families and as a church, we have grown in maturity in Christ.

So Paul exhorts, *"let us go on"*, like a sailing ship moving because it is blown by the wind. If you do not put your sail up, you will not be going anywhere. There has to be an agreement between what you do and what God says. God says that He will take us on, but we have to put up the sail. 'Going' on to perfection is 'being taken' on to perfection. It is God who wants to mature you. It is God who wants to perfect you; He wants to take you on to spiritual maturity. That is the will of God for each one of us. Note: **God will** carry us forward but we must work with Him, yield to Him and act in accordance with Him. You cannot make yourself mature. You cannot think it into being or act it into being. It is only realised by you recognizing the work of the Spirit, through the Word and through your times in prayer. If you are sensitive to Him and willing to listen to Him, He will make sure that you grow in this walk.

We need to yield to God:
i) **our wills:**
   You will need to make decisions, which are an act of your will, without which you will hinder your spiritual growth. The Spirit of God will draw your will to a place of decision and obedience if you allow Him.

ii) **our minds:**
   You need to exercise your mind. You need to study the Word. You need to read the Word and the Holy Spirit will bring all things back to your remembrance, but He cannot bring back to remembrance what was not there. That

promise means that you have studied God's Word. He says, "If you put it in, I will bring it back to your remembrance." I have seen in many situations over the years that when I have been in great need, the Spirit of God has raised up a scripture in my heart and in my mouth as a standard (flag) against the enemy. Without fail the very Scripture or truth that He raised up was always something I had previously studied and known.

iii) **affections and emotions:**

Bring your feelings, emotions and desires, under the will of God. These things can be the greatest hindrances to spiritual growth, yet when submitted unto God they become vital in moving forward in His will and purpose.

iv) **effort (diligence):**

We must put diligence and effort into spiritual growth. It does not happen miraculously overnight. Neither does it happen in passive saints. If you want to grow you must activate yourself spiritually. The Spirit of God will prompt us, challenge us, and guide us in arising and doing but we must be willing.

The goal is spiritual growth and maturity. The goal is to build a life which is mature in Jesus Christ—*"unto perfection."* The word *perfection* is the Greek word, *teleiotes* which means completeness or fulfilment. It is a state accomplished by a process.

In **Hebrews 2:10** and **5:9** we see that Christ was *"made perfect"* by the things He suffered. He was **made** *"perfect"*— that is wholly qualified—for His work as our High priest. Christ was not able to be our High Priest the way He was. He had to be born as a man. He had to take on flesh. He had to experience temptation like you and me. How could He be a good and effectual High Priest moved with compassion unless He had done so? You could have said, "He does not know what I am going through. He does not know what it means to be tempted." But He does, because He was tempted in every point even as we are. Christ was 'suited' and 'fitted' to the task. He was 'sinlessly perfect,' yet had to be made fit for this task. Now the 'Perfect One' wants to occupy our lives. Is it any wonder then that we have to go through a process of growth and maturing when it was necessary for Christ to do such? God is not going to change. You are going to have to change if you aim to fulfil what He has called you to. If you do not change, there are things that God will not be able to do in and through your life. This is reality.

We hear too often, "No one is perfect. God does not expect perfection." We hear, "Ah sure, we are all sinners saved by grace." But that is bringing everything down to our level. In Matthew 5:48, **Jesus Christ Himself** says, *"Be ye therefore perfect, even as your Father which is in heaven is perfect."* Perfect is the Greek word, *teleios,* which means to be complete, of full age and to be fully mature.

Now Christ is speaking to the Church here. Yes, God **expects perfection of you. There is no excuse for not being perfect.** No need to crumble in a bundle of condemnation. We are all growing, but do not justify being immature or not going on with Christ. In this verse we see that Christ has set the standard: the standard is our Father in Heaven. The standard is not set by any man, preacher, denomination or saint. The standard is set by Christ and that standard is God the Father. Seek to follow after our perfect Father in Heaven.

Christ is speaking to His Disciples here. Peter failed Him. Thomas doubted Him. Simon the zealot got all stirred up in the politics of the hour and was annoyed when Christ did not bring in a physical, political power, yet these are the frail men Christ is commanding to *'be ye perfect.'* We are not allowed to stay as babes. Of course you can ignore this calling and shut your ears to it but Christ is calling us ever onward to be true men and women of God, to stand up straight in this bending generation and to be spiritually mature in a church age that is terribly immature.

Perfection is a state of heart before God. We read of the following men who walked in perfection:

- **Noah:** The Bible says that, *"...Noah was a just and perfect man in his generation..."* (Gen.6:9). Note: this is pre-New Testament times and under the 'old dispensation'. This is before there was an indwelling Holy Spirit. This is before Calvary. This is before the wonderful written Canon of Scripture, yet Noah and these other men were perfect in their generation.

- **Job:** Job was a man that *"...was perfect and upright, and one that feared God, and eschewed evil"* (**1:1**). Job rejected evil; he went around it; he shunned evil and feared God. He was upright and righteous in all his dealings. This defines perfection.
- **Moses:** speaking to the whole nation of Israel said, *"Thou shalt be perfect with the LORD thy God"* (Deut. 18:13). So God required of Israel as a nation under the law to be perfect with the Lord and to grow up in a manner acceptable to Him.
- **David**: Did David ever fail God? Oh yes he did but that was not the mark of his life. In earlier years he himself said, *"I will behave myself wisely in a perfect way. O when wilt thou come to me? I will walk within my house with a perfect heart"* (Ps.101:2). David wanted to walk with a perfect heart, motives, thoughts, and desires. He did not want to have a double agenda or be insincere. David's life was marked by spiritual maturity and a depth of fellowship with the Lord. He had a heart after God that would not let him go down in laziness or carelessness.
- In the New Testament we read, *"[Christ] whom we preach, warning every man, and teaching every man in all wisdom; that we may present every man perfect in Christ Jesus"* (Col.1:28). *"Epaphras...always labouring fervently for you in prayers, that ye may stand perfect and complete in all the will of God"* (4:12). All true preaching and praying has this end in view to present individual believers and churches perfect or spiritually mature in Christ.

Paul, writing to the Colossians, wrote, *"Whom we preach, warning every man, and teaching every man in all wisdom; that we may present every man perfect in Christ Jesus"* (1:28). When you are saved you are made perfect in Christ Jesus through His perfect offering at Calvary, but Paul is talking about something else here. He is talking about an experience that genuine believers are to move into. He is saying that all of his preaching and warning is toward this end that he might present the Colossian church perfect, fully grown, in a state of genuine spiritual maturity. If you do not warn your child about running out into the street he will not grow up to maturity but will more than likely end up in a coffin. The preaching of God's Word and the preacher warning you and teaching you is God's way to protect you from being killed or at least stunted in your growth. When you are warned to stay a million miles away from 'the world', stay a million miles from that world. Every warning, challenge, and teaching is to that end of *presenting you perfect.*

Perfection is growing into Christ. Perfection is having your attitudes changed. Perfection is becoming like Christ and that your life would align with Jesus Christ.

Paul writes in Ephesians chapter four, about the five ministries given to the Body of Christ: *"And he gave some, apostles; and some, prophets; and some, evangelists; and some, pastors and teachers; For <u>the perfecting of the saints</u>...for the edifying of the body of Christ: Till we all come in the unity of the faith, and of the knowledge of the Son of God, <u>unto a perfect man</u>, <u>unto the measure of the stature of the fullness of Christ:</u> That we henceforth be no more **children,** tossed to and fro, and carried about with every wind of doctrine, by the sleight of men, and cunning craftiness, whereby they lie in wait to deceive; But speaking the truth in love, may <u>grow up into him</u> in all things, which is the head, even Christ"* (4:11-15). Preachers are given for your maturity.

Whilst you are in this physical body and on this Earth you are going to be on this journey of pressing onward and upward. Paul writes to the church at Philippi, *"Not as though I had already attained, either were already **perfect**: <u>but I</u> follow after, if that I may apprehend that for which also I am apprehended of Christ Jesus"* (3:12). Christ apprehended Paul, now Paul spends his life apprehending Christ, or *laying a hold of Christ*, in order to find out why Christ saved him and to allow that eternal plan for his life to come forth. Verse 15, *"...<u>Let us</u> therefore, **as many as be perfect**, be thus minded: and if in any thing ye be otherwise minded, God shall reveal even this unto you."* Notice now that the 'I' of verse 12, is now 'us' in verse 15. Paul was conscious that he was personally not yet perfect, by which he meant that he was not finished in his spiritual growth and maturing into the likeness of Jesus Christ, but at the very same time he states that there are those who are now enjoying a state of spiritual perfection in the churches and he counts himself amongst them.

So Paul says, I am perfect but I am not yet perfected.

How can you presently be perfect yet at the same time be pressing on towards perfection? Look at an apple tree. At the start of springtime, tiny apples, the size of a fingernail start to form from the bud, but later in the late summer and early autumn, we see a larger fruit ready for harvesting. That tiny apple is not fully grown in springtime but it is at a perfect stage for its stage of growth and the time of the year. Likewise, the larger apple later in the year is also perfect and exactly as it should be for that time of the year. This means you can be perfect at any stage of your growth yet pressing on to full maturity in Christ. As the Word of God has an effect on your life, you will grow from a perfect new-born babe to a mature perfect man in Christ Jesus. You will be in a state of perfection at birth but will be made perfect as you walk. Paul says that if you are not thinking correctly about going on to perfection, God will show you. God will convict you. Please be sure that the real Holy Spirit (when listened to) will always be urging you onwards to perfection and will never excuse your immaturity, foolishness, lightness, or laziness. Such things utterly contradict and hinder His purpose and will hinder Him and His work of maturing you.

If you are happy to stay the way you are then you are backslidden. Nobody stays static. You are either moving forward or you are moving back! If you are just holding your own, then you are losing ground. You must go somewhere. You are going to have to fight sin, fight demons, fight feelings, and fight through circumstances. Those athletes of ancient Greece only grew or developed their muscles as they exercised. The old Army saying of, "No pain, no gain," stands true today in the church. You must feel a burning in those muscles if the exercise is going to do you any good. If all you do is just manage the run and think, "My breathing is good, I don't feel any stretching, no muscle is aching, I won't push myself," you will not get any fitter. If you just manage a run, with hardly a sweat so that you look good, it will do you no good physically or spiritually. You need to press forward to the point of feeling burning muscles, stretched lungs, and sweating brow if you are to get fitter. You must not think, "I'm saved, so I can do whatever I want." You will damage yourself. You will retard yourself back to a baby stage. You will lose years or months or weeks of experience, teaching or preaching. A few 'stupid' spiritual decisions can put you right back and you will have to work through the elementary principles all over again to get back to where you ought to be.

Why does God want you to have a healthy spiritual experience and foundation where repentance is solidly laid, faith is steadfastly fixed upon God, with you baptized into the body of Christ and functioning in it, baptized in water, baptized in the Holy Ghost, regularly in an environment of local church ministry, where hands are laid on you and with confidence in a real resurrection of the dead and with a deep consciousness of eternal judgment? Because He wants to take you somewhere and that somewhere is perfect maturity in Christ and without the right foundation you will not be able to do so.

In an hour of terrible spiritual immaturity, laziness, worldliness, carnality and apostasy this book is a call for every believer and every church to go on to maturity and perfection in Jesus Christ. May you know the grace of God and the power of God's Holy Spirit enabling you to fulfil this vital call in this last hour of Church history.

Appendix i

PAUL THE PENMAN

This simple appendix is added for the purpose of clarifying and proving that Paul was the author of Hebrews. While settling this issue is not vital, or absolutely necessary to hearing the message contained in the book of Hebrews, I believe that it will help us in setting the letter in its context, and will open up the treasure of this great epistle with greater depth and meaning to our hearts. Before I present reasons why I believe that Paul was the author, I would like to note the most common arguments put forth against Paul being the author.

The Opposing View and a Response
Firstly, those opposed to Paul's authorship of this book say that it cannot be written by Paul because of the style of the Greek in which it is written. They believe that this book is written in a more professional style as opposed to the Greek used in all of Paul's other writings. They say that the Greek used in the letter to the Hebrews is more similar to that contained in the Gospel of Luke and the Book of Acts, rather than to Paul's writings in Ephesians or Romans.

However, over the years many great linguistic scholars have placed no weight in this argument although they do acknowledge the difference in the style. It is worth noting that it would seem that Paul frequently used a secretary to scribe a letter (Tertius was just one example: Rom.16:22), and his common practice seems to have been to then add a personal note in his own handwriting at the end of the dictated work (I Cor.16:21; Col.4:18; II Thess.3:17). Paul also mentions other brethren in eight of his letters from whom the letters are jointly sent. It would not be beyond possibility at all to consider that Luke was involved with writing Hebrews as Paul's secretary or scribe. What is of great interest is that almost all of those who suggest an alternative author for Hebrews almost always suggest one of his close associates or co-workers purely because it is impossible to believe that Hebrews does not carry some vital influence from Paul.

Secondly, those opposed to Paul's authorship of Hebrews, say that his name is not on it as on every other letter he wrote. In all of Paul's 13 acknowledged letters he always begins with: 'Paul, an apostle of Jesus Christ...' or 'Paul a servant of God...' or 'Paul, a prisoner...' yet in the letter to the Hebrews there is no such opening greeting. Rather, Hebrews starts with, *"God, who at sundry times and in divers manners spake in time past unto the fathers by the prophets, Hath in these last days spoken unto us by his Son, whom he hath appointed heir of all things, by whom also he made the worlds..."* (Heb.1:1-2). To support this further, they often quote, II Thessalonians 3:17-18, *"The salutation of Paul with mine own hand, which is the token in every epistle: so I write. The grace of our Lord Jesus Christ be with you all."* By this they infer that Paul himself stated that he placed his own name on each of his epistles as a token of his authorship and since his name does not appear anywhere on the letter to the Hebrews, they say that Paul cannot be the author.

In response to this I would like to point out that Paul does not state in this verse that he **scribes his name** on every letter. What he does say is that **he writes a** *"salutation"* at the end of each letter with his own hand, and this is his token. A 'salutation' is a warm greeting in words. We can see above that his salutation to the Thessalonians was, *"The grace of our Lord Jesus Christ be with you all."* This same 'salutation' (or something similar), appears in all of Paul's 13 epistles, but in no other book of the New Testament by any other author.

How does Hebrews finish? *"Grace be with you all. Amen"* (13:25). So, we clearly see that Hebrews actually does carry Paul's normal 'salutation' or token just as in all of his other writings.

Thirdly, those opposed to Paul's authorship of this book refer to Hebrews 2:3, *"How shall we escape, if we neglect so great salvation; which at the first began to be spoken by the Lord, and was confirmed unto us by them that heard him."* From this they surmise that it cannot be Paul writing as Paul received the gospel directly from Christ and was always very clear in his letters to the churches in stating that no other apostle had taught him the gospel (Gal.1:1, 11-12; 2:1-10). It is inferred that in this verse in Hebrews the author is acknowledging that he had received the gospel through the confirmation of the apostles who had personally heard Christ and so by this they state that Paul is disqualified from being the author of Hebrews.

In response to this I would first state that the author of Hebrews is not at all saying that he received the Gospel through the twelve apostles or that he came to faith through them. Neither is this statement given in reference to the preaching of salvation and the personal call to repent in a specific individual's life. The word *"confirmed"* used here means to make stable, steadfast or sure. It is a confirmation of something already received from Christ. Paul is writing to the Hebrews as a fellow countryman (he was a Hebrew of Hebrews). When he says it was confirmed *"to us"* he is saying it was confirmed to the Hebrew people. He is not talking as the apostle to the Gentiles; he is speaking as a Hebrew of the Hebrews who was mightily converted to Christ. The gospel that came by Christ was indeed confirmed to the nation of Israel by the apostles. Paul simply acknowledges this. Nothing in this statement contradicts that Christ personally met with Paul, and revealed the gospel to him (without the direct influence of the twelve apostles). It was about three years later that Paul first went to Jerusalem where the apostles did indeed acknowledge Paul's commission to the Gentiles (Gal.2:1, 7-9).

Proof
The first point I want to present in support of Paul writing this epistle, is Peter's comment in his second epistle: *"...our beloved brother Paul...hath written unto **you**; As also in all his epistles...in which are some things hard to be understood, which they that are unlearned and unstable wrest as they do also the other Scriptures unto their own destruction"* (II Pet.3:15-16). Peter wrote his two epistles to the Hebrew people who were scattered across diverse lands outside of Judea and yet still a recognised people. These people are known as 'scattered strangers' (Deut.4:7; Jn.7:35; Acts 2:8-11; Jm.1:1). *"Peter, an*

apostle of Jesus Christ, to the strangers scattered throughout Pontus, Galatia, Cappadocia, Asia, and Bithynia"—that is Asia Minor (I Pet.1:1). *"This second epistle, beloved, I now write unto you"* (II Pet.3:1). Both of his letters are written to the Hebrew people.

These letters were written to believers from a Jewish or Hebrew background scattered throughout these lands. Peter was not primarily writing to the Gentile Christians or churches. When referring to Paul he notes that Paul wrote to *"you"* just as he had written a number of other *"epistles."* He makes a distinction between this letter written to *"you"* and all his other writings which he groups together and calls *"all his epistles"* which obviously were not specifically written to *"you"* the Hebrews. According to Peter's statement Paul wrote a specific letter to Jewish or Hebrew-born Christians. But none of Paul's 13 epistles were written specifically to converted Hebrews either in Jerusalem or scattered across Asia Minor. We must look outside of Paul's 13 letters for this one written to these Hebrews and that leads us to ascertain that he was the author of the Book of Hebrews.

The second 'proof' of Paul's penmanship of this epistle arises in the thirteenth chapter of Hebrews when the author mentions Timothy: *"Know ye that our brother Timothy is set at liberty; with whom, if he come shortly, I will see you"* (Heb.13:23). Some state that it cannot be Paul writing here because he calls Timothy *"brother"* rather than *"son"* but we need only note that Paul calls Timothy *"brother"* in four different letters (II Cor.1:1; Col.1:1; I Thess.3:2; Philm.1:1). The author of Hebrews was waiting with hope that if Timothy came *"shortly"* both would pay a visit to the Hebrews. The only person in the New Testament who had such a relationship with Timothy was Paul. Not only does he imply friendship with him and companionship in ministry travels but also the ability to say Timothy would indeed come with him upon his return.

The third point regards the circumstances revealed concerning the author. After mentioning Timothy and before he closes his letter he sends greetings: *"Salute all them that have the rule over you, and all the saints. They of Italy salute you"* (13:24). The author was in Italy, in company with the saints probably in Rome, awaiting Timothy, and ready to pay a visit to the Hebrews in Christ. This fits Paul perfectly. This letter without doubt was written and sent between 60 AD and 70 AD and if we are correct maybe after 63 AD when Paul was released from prison and before the terrible persecution which began in the following year. The author of Hebrews mentions his imprisonment: *"For ye had compassion of me in my bonds"* (10:34). Also his *"salute"* to and from the saints was a normal statement used by Paul in his writings (Rom.16:5-22; I Cor.16:19; 13:13; Phil.4:21-22; Col.4:15; II Tim.4:19; Tit.3:15; Phm.1:23).

The fourth point to note, is the theme of the letter. The author is an expert in the Jewish culture, custom and law. He was on home ground when writing to the Hebrews. In Paul's formative years as a Christian, a preacher, and as a teacher he had literally wrestled out and lived out the fundamental themes and message set forth in the book of Hebrews. His radical conversion immediately faced him into the turmoil of wrestling through the issue of Old Testament Israel and the New Testament Church, with Christ as its High Priest. He had lived out the message and theology of this book like no man on Earth. Also in his opening comments in Hebrews the theme of Christ as the exclusive one that God speaks through, the one appointed heir of all things and as being the creator of all things were all the core themes of Paul's letters and the substance at the heart of his doctrinal teaching.

We could say much more in defence of Paul being the author of the book of Hebrews but we believe that the above comments are sufficient at least to answer any doubts and to build a solid foundation for further thorough research if any doubts remain. With us stands a great host of scholars, preachers, and leaders, both ancient and modern, (spanning the early second century until the present) who believe that Paul was the author of Hebrews. I recommend the reading of the introduction to Hebrews by Albert Barnes, in his commentary for a very good review and overview of the early churches acceptance of Paul as the author.

Having said all this we can afford to disagree or to be in doubt about the author but we must not doubt its inspiration by the Holy Ghost and we must not miss hearing, receiving and obeying the message contained within it for this is the most vital thing of all. These comments are placed here for your help and learning not for any purpose of argument. May we always be willing to listen to a fellow brother and to weigh his words in the light of scripture avoiding controversy and contention at all costs.

Divine Inspiration

Let us close this short appendix by thinking of the divine inspiration that is claimed for this letter when we accept Paul as its author and the comments Peter makes concerning it. *"...our beloved brother Paul...hath written unto you; As also in all his epistles...in which are some things hard to be understood, which they that are unlearned and unstable wrest as they do also the other Scriptures unto their own destruction"* (II Pet.3:15-16).

This certainly shows us that at this stage Paul's letters were already well known to the church, both Jewish and Gentile, and were known, read and acknowledged by Peter. This is some years after Paul's conflict with Peter which we read of in Galatians 2. It is so beautiful to see Peter speak of *"our beloved brother Paul."* Both of these men had been reconciled for some years now. We see by this that without argument they were clearly writing and preaching the same message and Gospel in utter agreement and that Peter was strong in commending Paul.

Peter goes on to speak further of Paul's writings, *"...in which"*—this *refers* to the letter from Paul to the Hebrews— *"...are some things hard to be understood, which they that are unlearned and unstable wrest* [twist]*, as they do also the **other Scriptures.**"* That word *"scriptures"* is only used by the Jews concerning the divinely inspired Word of God. In the New Testament this term is used when speaking of the Old Testament writings. The scriptures were writings that were inspired, or breathed out by God through a human vessel. In verse 15 he states clearly that Paul *"according to the wisdom given unto him hath written unto you."* Peter knew that it was by wisdom given from God that Paul wrote and not his own wisdom or intellectual learning. Peter places Paul's letters on a par with the Old Testament scriptures, acknowledging their inspiration by the

Holy Spirit. It is of great interest that when Paul wrote to Timothy he uses a quote from the Old Testament and a quote from the Gospel of Luke and calls them both Scripture (Lk.10:7; I Tim.5:18). It seems that before the close of the apostolic age and the death of the first apostles that they had already accepted those writings which were inspired of God for the churches amongst which was this one written to the Hebrews (I Pet.1:12).

A popular trend in today's Church seeks to undermine who Paul was and what he wrote. Many would prefer it if they could prove that 'Paul got it wrong' yet here we have the apostle Peter saying that Paul's letters were not the writings of 'just a man' but were divinely inspired by the Holy Spirit sent down from heaven. Every letter which Paul wrote was God writing, breathing through His chosen penman. If we are weak in conviction of the *Divine inspiration of Scripture*, we will be weak in every other area. You will never be settled on any issue if you think it is just man writing these letters. It is the Holy Spirit of God using a human vessel. This also reveals that the writings of Paul were not only for the Gentile converts but also for the Hebrew converts. The converted Hebrews, just like Peter, accepted Paul's writings as authoritive and from God.

He goes on to say that in them, *"are some things hard to be understood* [hard to be uttered or hard to be explained], *which they that are unlearned and unstable wrest* [twist]*."* Here Peter is saying that when Paul gets to writing or teaching, there are some things not easily understood with the natural mind.

Peter is not saying that Paul should change his style of preaching, teaching or letter writing. Peter is not complaining or requiring that Paul should use different words or phraseology. Neither is Peter suggesting that Paul should move on from complicated doctrines. NO! Peter is saying that some things which Paul teaches in his letters are things with which one has to wrestle, labour and pray in order to understand. There is an expectation here that we must grow to a place of maturity and understanding in the knowledge of the written scriptures. There is an expectation that we will have to grapple with these things *"hard to be understood."*

Saints, you are going to have to use your mind. You are going to have to spend time and pray over things *'hard to be understood'*. The richest things we find in the earth are buried deep in the ground. You will have to dig deep to mine for gold. The most precious truths in the Bible are going to have to be studied—you will have to use your mind. Paul's letters may be *hard to be understood on the surface* but you will have to dig in order to understand them. We may well have the revelation of Christ as Saviour and we may well have experienced the new birth; we may well be on our way to heaven with sufficient knowledge but there are a wealth of truths in the Bible which we are going to have to study if we are to comprehend them. We must *"study to show ourselves approved"* (II Tim 2:15).

Bulk orders of this book may be obtained directly from the author at a reduced price

14857605R00107

Printed in Great Britain
by Amazon.co.uk, Ltd.,
Marston Gate.